W9-CJC-306

PUBLIC LIBRARY DISTRICT OF COLUMBIA

Steck-Vaughn

GED

SCIENCE
Exercise Book

READING LEVEL
CATEGORY
WORKBOOK AVAILABLE
TCHER. GUIDE AVAILABLE
PART OF A SERIES
OUT OF PRINT
CASSETTE AVAILABLE

STECK-VAUGHN
ELEMENTARY · SECONDARY · ADULT · LIBRARY

A Harcourt Company

ACKNOWLEDGMENTS

Executive Editor: Ellen Northcutt
Senior Editor: Donna Townsend
Associate Design Director: Joyce Spicer
Supervising Designer: Pamela Heaney

Photo Credits: Cover: (lightning) ©Kent Wood/Photo Researchers, Inc., (red-eyed tree frog) ©Tim Davis/Photo Researchers, Inc., (space station) Courtesy NASA; p.i. ©Kent Wood/Photo Researchers, Inc.

ISBN 0-7398-3602-1

Copyright © 2002 Steck-Vaughn Company

All rights reserved. No part of the material protected by this copyright may be reproduced or utilized in any form or by any means, electronic or mechanical, including photocopying, recording, or by any information storage and retrieval system, without permission in writing from the copyright owner. Requests for permission to make copies of any part of the work should be mailed to: Copyright Permissions, Steck-Vaughn Company, P.O. Box 26015, Austin, Texas 78755.

Printed in the United States of America.

9 10 11 073 08 07 06 05

Contents

To the Learner 2

Unit 1: Life Science 4

Unit 2: Earth and Space Science 21

Unit 3: Physical Science 32

Simulated GED Test A 50

Analysis of Performance: Test A............................69

Simulated GED Test B 70

Analysis of Performance: Test B............................89

Answers and Explanations...............................90

Answer Sheet...110

The *Steck-Vaughn GED Science Exercise Book* provides you with practice in answering the types of questions found on the actual GED Science Test. It can be used with the *Steck-Vaughn GED Science* book or with the *Steck-Vaughn Complete GED Preparation* book. This exercise book contains both practice exercises and simulated GED tests.

Practice Exercises

The GED Science Test examines your ability to understand, apply, analyze, and evaluate information in three science areas. The practice exercises are divided into the same three content areas by unit. Life science examines living things and how they interact with each other and their environment. This area covers plant and animal biology, including human body systems and health. Earth and space science examines Earth, the solar system, and the universe. Physical science includes chemistry—the study of matter and changes in matter—and physics—the study of the interrelationships of matter and energy, including heat, light, sound, electricity, magnetism, atomic reactions, and motion.

Simulated Tests

This exercise contains complete full-length Simulated GED Science Tests. Each Simulated Test has the same number of items as the GED Test. In addition, each test provides practice with item types similar to those found on the GED Test. The Simulated Tests can help you decide if you are ready to take the GED Science Test. To benefit most from the Simulated Tests, take each test under the same time restrictions as you will have for the actual GED Test. For each test, complete the 50 items within 80 minutes. Space the two examinations apart by at least a week.

Question Types

The GED Science Test is divided into three content areas: life science, Earth and space science, and physical science.

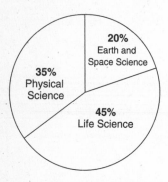

On the GED Science Test, a graphic or a reading passage is followed by one question or several related questions. Forty-five percent of the questions are about life science, 20 percent are about Earth and space science, and 35 percent are about physical science. Many of the questions focus on science that is relevant to daily life, such as environmental and health topics. All the questions on the GED Science Test are multiple-choice. You will not be tested on your knowledge of science, but rather on your ability to understand and analyze science concepts and to apply them in problem-solving situations. Half of the questions on the test are problem-solving questions. Following is an explanation of the four types of questions that you will practice in this book and that are found on the GED Test.

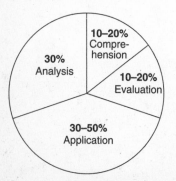

1. Comprehension questions require you to identify restated information or information that is paraphrased. They require you to summarize ideas or identify implications.

2. Application questions require you to apply a principle or concept and make a prediction of what would happen in a similar instance. They require you to use the information provided to solve a problem in a new context.

3. Analysis questions require you to classify information. Sometimes you will be asked to distinguish or compare and contrast information presented.
4. Evaluation questions test your ability to identify opinions and recognize assumptions. Other evaluation items ask you to identify cause and effect relationships.

On the GED Science Test, 10–20% of the items are comprehension, 30–50% are application, 30% are analysis, and 10–20% are evaluation. In addition, these four types of questions integrate content included in the National Science Education Standards: fundamental understandings, unifying concepts and processes, science as inquiry, science and technology, science in personal and social perspectives, and the history and nature of science.

Graphics

Approximately one-third of the items relate to a drawing, chart, map, or graph. Practice with graphics is essential to develop the skills to interpret information presented on the GED Science Test. Always read the title, key, and any other information associated with the illustration before answering any questions.

Answers

The answer section gives explanations of why an answer is correct, and why the other answer choices are incorrect. Sometimes by studying the reason an answer is incorrect, you can learn to avoid a similar problem in the future.

Analysis of Performance Charts

After each Simulated Test, an Analysis of Performance Chart will help you determine if you are ready to take the GED Science Test. The charts give a breakdown by content area (life science, Earth and space science, and physical science) and by question type (comprehension, application, analysis, and evaluation). By completing these charts, you can determine your own strengths and weaknesses as they relate to the science area.

Correlation Chart

The following correlation chart shows how the sections of this exercise book relate to sections of other Steck-Vaughn GED preparation books. You can refer to these two books for further instruction or review.

CONTENT AREAS	Life Science	Earth and Space Science	Physical Science
BOOK TITLES *Steck-Vaughn GED Science Exercise Book*	Unit 1	Unit 2	Unit 3
Steck-Vaughn GED Science	Unit 1	Unit 2	Unit 3
Steck-Vaughn Complete GED Preparation	Unit 4, Life Science	Unit 4, Earth and Space Science	Unit 4, Physical Science

UNIT 1 Life Science

Directions: Choose the <u>one best answer</u> to each question.

<u>Question 1</u> refers to the following diagram.

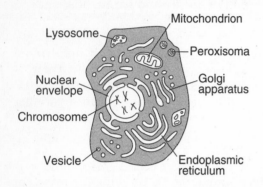

1. Based on the above diagram, which of the following cell structures occurs within the cell nucleus?

   (1) vesicle
   (2) mitochondrion
   (3) chromosome
   (4) Golgi apparatus
   (5) lysosome

<u>Question 2</u> refers to the following information.

An inherited trait or behavior is one that is passed on through the genes from parents to offspring.
A learned trait is not passed on genetically, but is taught to the offspring by the parents.

2. Which of the following is an inherited trait of humans?

   (1) the ability to learn a language
   (2) hunting prowess
   (3) knowledge of agriculture
   (4) the ability to speak Spanish
   (5) skill at playing an instrument

<u>Question 3</u> refers to the following information and diagram.

Stomata (singular: stoma) are epidermal pores, or openings, found on the underside of a plant's leaves. They regulate the exchange of gases and water vapor between the leaf and the atmosphere. Each of the stomata is surrounded by two guard cells that swell and relax to control the size of the opening. For example, on a very hot, dry day, the guard cells may keep the stomata closed to prevent water from escaping from the plant.

Guard Cells

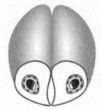

Stoma closed   Stoma open

3. Based on the passage and the diagram, what is the function of a plant's guard cells?

   (1) to filter out strong light
   (2) to take in water
   (3) to take in oxygen for photosynthesis
   (4) to regulate temperature
   (5) to regulate the opening and closing of the stomata

Question 4 refers to the following information and diagram.

The axon is an extended portion of a nerve cell (or neuron) that transmits sensory stimuli in the form of an electrical signal. The electrical signal travels from the central portion of the nerve cell along the axon and is transmitted to the next neuron. The axon is sheathed in layers of glial cells. These cells form a membrane that protects the axon and keeps the electrical signal intact.

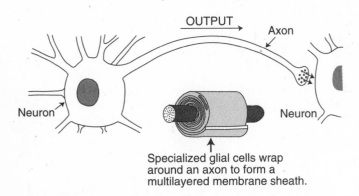

Specialized glial cells wrap around an axon to form a multilayered membrane sheath.

4. Which of the following has the same function as the sheath of glial cells?

   (1) the case around lipstick
   (2) the wood around a graphite pencil
   (3) the thermos holding hot coffee
   (4) the insulation around electric wire
   (5) the glass around a light bulb filament

Question 5 refers to the following passage.

The English peppered moth lives in northern England. About 150 years ago, the bark of the trees on which the moths rested was covered with light-colored lichen. Most of the moths were the same color as the lichen, so they were camouflaged perfectly. Their coloration made them nearly invisible to the birds that would otherwise eat them.

When heavy industry took over in the northern part of England, pollution from factories killed the lichen, exposing the dark brown tree bark. Birds who preyed on the English peppered moths could now spot the light-colored insects easily. Many light-colored moths were eaten. But the few English peppered moths that carried the gene for a darker color were not eaten. Camouflaged on the dark bark, they survived to reproduce and pass on the gene for dark color to their offspring. Soon the dark-colored variety of English peppered moths became far more common than the light-colored ones in polluted areas.

5. Which of the following behaviors or processes does the above passage describe?

   (1) hibernation
   (2) natural selection
   (3) predation
   (4) industrialization
   (5) migration

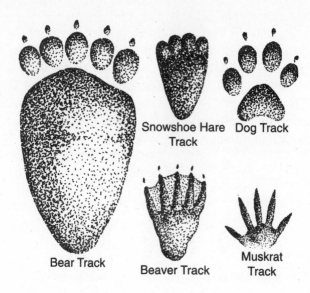

6. Which tracks show evidence of toenails?

    (1) bear, muskrat, beaver
    (2) bear, dog, beaver
    (3) snowshoe hare, dog, muskrat
    (4) beaver, muskrat
    (5) snowshoe hare, muskrat

7. Which animal's track <u>most</u> closely resembles a human footprint?

    (1) beaver
    (2) bear
    (3) snowshoe hare
    (4) dog
    (5) muskrat

8. Using the beaver's track as a reference, what is one characteristic that would most assist the beaver in building its house midstream?

    (1) number of toes
    (2) length of toes
    (3) webbing between the toes
    (4) absence of pads
    (5) absence of toes

9. From observation of the muskrat tracks, what is the <u>most likely</u> place to find its burrow?

    (1) junctions of tree branches
    (2) midstream
    (3) a factory chimney
    (4) soft soil
    (5) high hollows of trees

10. Assuming the tracks are drawn to scale, which of the following statements is supported by the illustrations?

    (1) Snowshoe hares live in forests.
    (2) Muskrats eat fish.
    (3) Beavers are larger than muskrats.
    (4) Beavers are related to dogs.
    (5) Snowshoe hares have five toes on their front feet.

Animals are killed chiefly for their meat. Leather is a by-product derived from the skins of those animals. To obtain lasting, flexible, attractive leather from hides involves a series of chemical processes. The skins are soaked in brine (salt water) to kill bacteria that naturally rot and decay the hides. They are then dried and scraped to remove any remaining fat, flesh, or dirt and soaked in a solution of slaked lime and sodium sulfide to loosen the hairs. A rinse of pancreatic extract and ammonia removes the lime.

The hides are then tanned (processed into leather) using an extract of hemlock or oak tree bark called tannin, which prevents further decay by bacteria. Various dyes are used to color the leather, which is then oiled with castor bean or cod liver oil. When dry, lacquers or waxes are painted on the leather to give it a shine and to prevent moisture and bacteria from entering the leather.

11. From raw material to product, which of the following materials would be processed most like leather?

  (1) pelts to fur coats
  (2) wood to paper
  (3) plant juices to ink
  (4) plant fibers to nylon
  (5) petroleum to gasoline

12. What is the most likely reason that protests against the use of animal skins for leather are not as intense as protests against skins for fur coats?

  (1) The skins for leather are a by-product from animals that have already been killed for their meat.
  (2) People have always used leather; whereas, the use of furs is a recent development.
  (3) The animals suffer more when killed for fur.
  (4) The animals used for leather are not as beautiful as those used for furs.
  (5) Coats can be made of cloth; whereas, the manufacture of footwear requires leather.

13. Very few people are allergic to animal skin; however, many individuals are allergic to leather. Which of the following explanations would most likely be the cause of the allergies?

  (1) Leather is not a living substance.
  (2) In leather, the hairs have been removed.
  (3) Chemicals used in processing leather cause the allergy.
  (4) The allergy is psychological, meaning sufferers object to killing animals to obtain leather.
  (5) Bacteria living on the leather cause the allergy.

Question 14 refers to the following passage.

Many illnesses are caused by foreign organisms, such as bacteria or viruses, that invade the body. The body's immune system can identify cells that are foreign and is designed to attack and kill any that enter the body. Although the immune system is crucial to survival, it is an obstacle to patients who have had an organ transplant. The immune system identifies the new organ as foreign and begins to attack and kill its cells.

14. Which of the following would help prevent the rejection of a transplanted organ?

  (1) getting an organ from a relative
  (2) taking drugs that suppress the patient's immune system
  (3) taking drugs that kill the cells in the patient's new organ
  (4) injecting bacteria into the patient
  (5) injecting viruses into the patient

Question 15 refers to the following graph.

Peach and Apple Orchard Yields

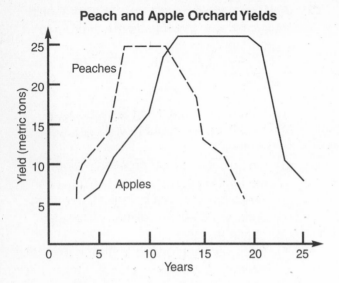

15. The graph gives information on which of the following considerations regarding fruit production?

    (1) the approximate size of the trees before fruit production begins
    (2) the approximate length of time the trees yield the most fruit
    (3) the approximate size of the trees when fruit production ceases
    (4) information to indicate that peak production of apples will fall off before that of peaches
    (5) data regarding the production of oranges in metric tons

---

Questions 16 through 22 refer to the following passage.

Pollination is the first step in a flowering plant's reproduction. In order to produce a seed that can become a new individual, the plant needs to flower. Delayed or premature flowering often results in diminished seed quality. In general, healthy seeds come from healthy plants.

Flowers contain male and/or female structures. Male structures produce pollen, which contains the sperm. The female structures have ovules, which contain the eggs. Flowers of tomato and pepper plants contain both male and female structures. Melons, squash, and cucumbers have some flowers that are male and other flowers that are female on the same plant. Pussy willows and papayas have only male flowers on one plant and female flowers on another plant.

Regardless of where the male and female structures are located, there can be no fruit, and subsequently no seeds, unless the sperm in the pollen reaches the ovules. Wind, insects, bats, birds, moths, and butterflies assist plants in the transfer of pollen to the female structure. A flower's colored petals, scent, and nectar are devices for attracting these natural agents of pollination. In situations where the natural transfer agents are missing, humans can assist plants.

16. Which of the following is a natural agent of pollination?

    (1) humans
    (2) flowers
    (3) nectar
    (4) seeds
    (5) wind

17. The flowers of wild grasses are often small and have no petals, scent, or nectar. Which of the following is probably the agent of pollination for most wild grasses?

    (1) humans
    (2) moths
    (3) insects
    (4) bats
    (5) wind

18. The label on a fruit-producing plant at a nursery says the plant won't produce fruit if there is only one in your yard. What can you infer about how this plant reproduces?

    (1) Male and female flowers grow on separate plants.
    (2) Both male flowers and female flowers grow on the same plant.
    (3) All the flowers have both male and female structures.
    (4) Humans must pollinate the plant.
    (5) The plant doesn't reproduce by flowers.

19. What is the function of flowers?

To

(1) increase the beauty of the plant
(2) notify people when plants need fertilizer
(3) indicate a plant's need for water
(4) provide the plants with more nutrition
(5) produce the reproductive elements necessary for seed formation

20. What is the best assurance that seeds will become healthy new plants?

(1) The flowers have both male and female structures.
(2) Pollen has reached the female element.
(3) The fruits for nourishment are large.
(4) The female element produces many ovules.
(5) The parent plant is healthy.

21. What is the most likely place humans would need to assist in pollination?

(1) on large farms of one crop type
(2) with nonflowering plants
(3) in desert or drought conditions
(4) in a commercial greenhouse
(5) in a backyard flower garden

22. Most moths fly only at night. They are guided by their sense of smell and by their sense of sight. Therefore, which of the following most likely describes moth-pollinated flowers?

(1) large and brightly colored
(2) large, white, and fragrant
(3) small, white, and odorless
(4) small, brightly colored, and fragrant
(5) open only during the day

23. The small dents on the surface of potatoes are called eyes. Each eye can sprout by producing a bud which can become a new plant. How are potato farmers most likely to start new plants?

By

(1) spreading seeds
(2) planting runners from mother plants
(3) placing the flowers from female plants in water to root
(4) cutting a potato into sections each having at least one eye, and then planting the sections
(5) plowing under the stem and leaves of old plants

Question 24 refers to the following illustration.

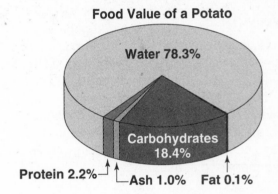

Food Value of a Potato

Water 78.3%

Carbohydrates 18.4%

Protein 2.2%

Ash 1.0%   Fat 0.1%

24. If all the water is removed from a 100-gram potato to make dried potato flakes, how much will the flakes weigh?

(1)   2.2 grams
(2) 18.4 grams
(3) 21.7 grams
(4) 78.3 grams
(5) 81.6 grams

25. A giraffe's long neck is an adaptation that enables it to utilize a food resource (treetop leaves) few other animals in its grassland habitat can use. Because it improves their chances in the competition for food resources, this adaptation helps giraffes survive.

Which of the following is also an adaptation that helps an animal utilize a food resource?

(1) kangaroo's pouch
(2) peacock's feathers
(3) hummingbird's long bill
(4) Arctic hare's white fur
(5) sheep's herding behavior

26. In 2000, scientists announced the completion of the first goal of the U.S. Human Genome Project. This goal was to identify and map each of the thousands of genes that make up the human genetic code. In the next stages of research, scientists will explore the function of each gene. Doctors say that one important outcome of this research will be the development of new medical applications. More and more, the science of genetics plays an important role in the diagnosis and treatment of diseases.

Scientists working on the Human Genome Project identified and mapped the human genome by analyzing which of the following?

(1) hemoglobin
(2) viruses
(3) white blood cells
(4) DNA
(5) cell nuclei

27. In 1995, students on a field trip to a farm pond found a large number of frogs with deformities. Some frogs had extra limbs, while others had misshapen or missing limbs. Since 1995, reports of frogs with deformities have become increasingly common. Some biologists believe that the increase in frog deformities is caused by environmental pollutants, and warn that humans should act quickly to identify and correct the problem.

Which of the following statements can be inferred from the information in the passage?

(1) Frogs are an important food source.
(2) What is happening to frogs will soon happen to humans.
(3) Birds that eat frogs may disappear.
(4) Frogs are more susceptible to environmental changes than other organisms.
(5) Humans may get diseases from deformed frogs.

28. A PET (Positron Emission Tomography) scan uses x-ray technology to visualize the brain. A person receiving a PET scan is injected with a substance that attaches itself to glucose and certain other chemicals in the brain. The x-rays track these substances as they move through the brain or are used by the body in certain processes. Because these processes are often related to brain diseases and disorders, PET scans are useful in diagnosing medical problems. Scans have also been used to visualize the brain during different activities or emotional states. This helps scientists understand how brain activity differs between a person with normal brain activity and one with brain damage.

Which of the following medical problems might require a PET scan?

(1) heart attack
(2) diabetes
(3) head trauma
(4) broken arm
(5) spinal cord injury

Question 29 refers to the following passage.

In 1989, hundreds of people became ill after taking a dietary supplement containing tryptophan, an amino acid. About 1500 cases, including 38 deaths, were reported to the Centers for Disease Control and Prevention. Banning the sale of tryptophan until they could research the problem, the Food and Drug Administration (FDA) began to test the health effects of these dietary supplements containing tryptophan. Concerned about its potentially negative effects, the FDA now restricts use of tryptophan.

29. Based on the above passage, what information should you have before you buy and use dietary supplements?

You should know if they

(1) are derived from organic sources
(2) come from plants
(3) have been tested for safety
(4) require a doctor's prescription
(5) work as advertised

Question 30 refers to the following passage.

In many zoos around the world, zoologists breed animals that are endangered. Captive breeding is a way of saving endangered species from extinction. The goal of many captive breeding programs is to release a population of animals back into the wild, where the animals would reproduce on their own, allowing the population to grow.

30. Which of the following statements identifies a captive breeding problem that may prevent programs from achieving their goal?

(1) Many species become extinct before scientists identify them.
(2) Most species on the brink of extinction are insects.
(3) Captive breeding programs do not take into account endangered plants.
(4) Most endangered species' habitats in the wild have been destroyed.
(5) There aren't enough endangered species to justify captive breeding programs.

Question 31 refers to the following information and graph.

The graph below shows the effect of repeated injections of the same antigen. The injections stimulate the production of antibodies. The bottom of the graph indicates the time intervals of the injections. The quantity of antibody produced increases over time until it reaches its maximum level.

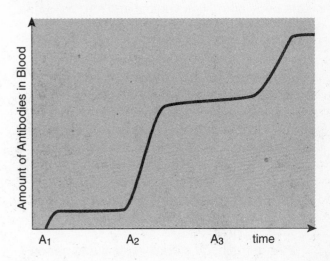

31. Based on the graph, at which point is the greatest amount of antibodies produced?

(1) before A_1
(2) between A_1 and A_2
(3) after A_2
(4) before A_3
(5) after A_3

Questions 32 through 34 refer to the following information.

Keys are used by biologists to classify and identify plants and animals. When using a key, a person always starts at the top and answers yes or no to the first qualifying question.

A person trying to identify Fish E would first ask if the fish is saucer-shaped. If the answser is no, the second question is asked. Are the stripes on the body of the fish vertical and narrow? If the answer is yes, the arrow identifies the fish as a zebra fish.

If a person knows the name of a fish and wishes to determine if a sample is that fish, identification is positive when the person answers yes to the question with the arrow pointing to the name and no to all the questions that precede it. Following is an example of the process.

(1) Is the fish saucer-shaped?
    If yes → stingray
    If no, go to 2.
(2) Are the body stripes vertical and narrow?
    If yes → zebra fish
    If no, go to 3.
(3) Is the mouth near the bottom of the head?
    If yes → scorpion fish
    If no, go to 4.
(4) Is there a lateral horizontal stripe parallel to the dorsal (top) fin?
    If yes → weever fish
    If no, go to 5.
(5) Are there vertical stripes on the caudal (tail) fin?
    If yes → stonefish

Fish A:

Fish B: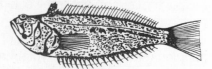

Fish C: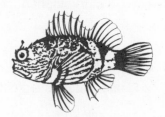

Fish D: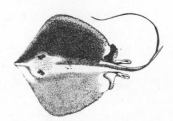

Fish E:

32. Using the classification key, which of the following is Fish D?

    A

    (1) stingray
    (2) zebra fish
    (3) scorpion fish
    (4) weever fish
    (5) stonefish

33. Using the classification key, which of the following is Fish B?

    A

    (1) stingray
    (2) zebra fish
    (3) scorpion fish
    (4) weever fish
    (5) stonefish

34. Using the classification key, which letter identifies a scorpion fish?

    (1) A
    (2) B
    (3) C
    (4) D
    (5) E

Questions 35 through 38 refer to the following table.

Uses of the Camel by Desert People

Transport	carry heavy loads
	plow fields
	turn water wheels
	transport humans
Food	milk, butter, cheese, and meat
Fibers	camel-hair clothing and blankets
Skin	leather shoes, water bags, and tents
Bones	carved utensils and jewelry
Droppings	fuel for warmth and cooking

35. Which of the following statements describes the survival of desert people in some areas of Africa and Asia?

    They are

    (1) threatened by the overpopulation of camels
    (2) threatened by competition with camels
    (3) dependent on the products and services of camels
    (4) dependent on the elimination of camels
    (5) independent of camels

36. Contrary to common belief, camels do not carry water in their humps. The humps contain fat, which in time of limited food supply is turned into water and sugar. When is a camel's hump likely to be largest?

    When the

    (1) female is pregnant
    (2) male is used to plow fields or carry loads
    (3) water supply is abundant
    (4) food supply is abundant
    (5) camel is young

37. What is the effect of the fact that camels sweat very little?

    It increases their

    (1) need for water
    (2) need for salt
    (3) ability to spit when angered
    (4) ability to survive in dry climates
    (5) capacity to reproduce

38. Camels have three eyelids over each eye. Which of the following is a likely function of this adaptation?

    To

    (1) keep the eyes dry
    (2) prevent sand from entering during sandstorms
    (3) sleep better at night
    (4) see better in the daytime
    (5) appear blind to its enemies

Question 39 refers to the following passage.

Many weeds in the United States were brought here as seeds by colonists who grew them for medicines, seasonings, pest control, cosmetics, scents, and dyes. As the production of chemical products was taken over by large companies, many of these prized plants were neglected and came to be viewed as weeds.

39. Which of the following statements best represents the main idea of the paragraph above?

    (1) Once a weed, always a weed.
    (2) All of America's weeds are foreign born.
    (3) Weeds are America's best source of chemicals.
    (4) Many of today's weeds were the prized plants of colonists.
    (5) Weeds have many uses in today's world.

40. Many methods are used to control weeds. Which of the following methods of weed control is unsafe for a food crop?

    (1) quarantine laws with inspection at ports of entry
    (2) inspection of commercial seeds for limits on the kind and percent of weed seeds contained
    (3) hoeing and cultivating
    (4) placing plastic sheeting, heavy paper, or mulch around plants
    (5) heavy spraying with unregulated chemicals that poison weeds

Questions 41 through 44 refer to the following illustration.

Punnett Square Showing the Cross Tt X Tt

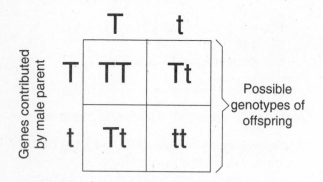

Genes contributed by female parent

Genes contributed by male parent

Possible genotypes of offspring

41. Which genotypes do the parents in the genetic cross shown in the diagram have?

    (1) Tt and Tt
    (2) TT and tt
    (3) Tt and TT
    (4) tt and tt
    (5) TT and TT

42. In the cross shown, the gene T is dominant over the gene t. If the cross produces 12 offspring, how many of them are likely to show the dominant trait, T?

    (1) 10
    (2) 9
    (3) 8
    (4) 3
    (5) 1

43. What are the most likely results of a cross between parents with genotypes Tt and tt?

    (1) all TT
    (2) all tt
    (3) all Tt
    (4) half Tt and half tt
    (5) one-fourth tt and three-fourths Tt

44. Many inherited human diseases, such as Tay-Sachs disease and sickle cell anemia, are caused by a recessive gene. A person born with one copy of the gene is a carrier. A person born with two copies of the gene has the disease.

Which of the following couples has a chance of having a child with sickle cell anemia?

    (1) a man who is a sickle cell carrier and a woman who is not
    (2) a woman who is a sickle cell carrier and a man who is not
    (3) two sickle cell carriers
    (4) a man who has sickle cell anemia and a woman who is not a sickle cell carrier
    (5) two people who do not carry sickle cell anemia

45. Desert plants must have structures to keep water in; whereas marshland plants must have structures to keep water out. Which of the following adaptations would serve both desert and marshland plants?

    (1) spines and thorns
    (2) thin, transparent skin
    (3) thick, tough skin
    (4) big flowers
    (5) many leaves

46. There is really no reason to be concerned about the reduction in stratospheric ozone. It is true that the ozone layer blocks out harmful ultraviolet (UV) rays from the sun, and that exposure to ultraviolet rays is known to cause skin cancer. But if you are careful, you can avoid overexposure to sunlight and thus prevent skin cancer from occurring.

On which of the following topics does the above argument need information in order to support its conclusions?

    (1) the amount of exposure to UV rays that causes skin cancer
    (2) the types of skin cancer that are treatable
    (3) other causes of skin cancer
    (4) how to apply sunscreen
    (5) the different types of UV rays

Questions 47 through 49 refer to the following information.

The only sugar that body cells can burn for energy is the simple sugar glucose. The sugar in foods we eat is rarely glucose. Some sugars and their sources are listed below.

Simple Sugars
    glucose—blood plasma
    fructose—fruits
Double Sugars
    maltose—grains and seeds
    sucrose—beets and cane (table sugar)

In the digestive process, the body breaks down double sugars into simple sugars and then changes all simple sugars to glucose before releasing them to the cells for energy.

Human Digestion of Sucrose

47. Which of the following statements is suggested in the information?

(1) Sucrose is a simple sugar.
(2) Sucrose must be broken down before body cells can use the energy.
(3) The sugar in fruits goes directly to cells without being changed to glucose.
(4) Beets contain maltose.
(5) The sugar in grains is called sucrose.

48. Which of the chemicals listed below is <u>most likely</u> a sugar?

(1) hydrochloric acid
(2) ammonia
(3) mannose
(4) magnesium hydroxide
(5) glue

49. When manufacturers of candy and heavy-syrup products list a package's ingredients, the chemical names for sugar are used. Many people who wish to control body weight are advised to limit sugar intake. Most people do not recognize the chemical names of sugars. What is the <u>most likely</u> result of this gap of knowledge by the general public?

Many consumers

(1) assume the products have no sugar
(2) buy the products because they sound scientific
(3) do not purchase the product because they are unsure of the ingredients
(4) find their weight unaffected by excessive intake
(5) refuse to buy the products until the Food and Drug Administration forces the manufacturers to use common names

50. Microorganisms living in the stomachs of ruminants (animals that chew a cud, such as cows) change the sugar of cellulose to glucose that the ruminant can then digest. Cellulose is found in grass and many plant fibers. Humans are unable to obtain glucose from cellulose.

What can you infer from this information?

(1) Cows have a more highly developed digestive system than humans.
(2) Humans must take vitamins in order to digest glucose.
(3) Cellulose is the sugar used by the cells of ruminants to obtain energy.
(4) The microorganisms that digest cellulose do not live in the human digestive system.
(5) Ruminants cannot digest fructose, sucrose, or maltose whereas humans can.

Question 51 refers to the following illustration.

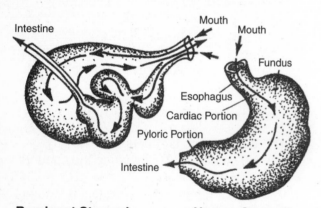

Ruminant Stomach   **Human Stomach**

51. When contrasting the ruminant stomach to the human stomach, the ruminant stomach has which of the following?

(1) smaller chambers
(2) fewer chambers
(3) a longer food route
(4) one food route
(5) a single pouch

Question 52 refers to the following passage.

When Charles Darwin visited the Galapagos Islands, he noticed various species of finches. The birds were very much alike, but each species had a beak with a different shape. All of the species had descended from a single species of finch that had been carried by winds to the remote islands. Darwin asked himself why the original, single finch species had become several different species. Darwin looked closely at the birds' beaks and their various shapes and sizes. He watched the birds and saw that each species ate different kinds of foods. After thinking about his findings, Darwin decided that the different species had evolved to exploit different food resources. Without competition for the same food resource, each species had a better chance of survival. From these insights, Darwin developed his theories of natural selection and evolution.

52. Which of the following key elements of scientific inquiry did Darwin use in his study of the finches?

(1) trial and error
(2) controlled laboratory experiments
(3) reproducing previous field work
(4) working only with a proven hypothesis
(5) careful observation

"Mad cow disease," or BSE (bovine spongiform encephalopathy), is a brain-wasting illness that is always fatal. Scientists are aware of how the disease is transmitted to cattle—through animal feed that contains infected animal parts. Though the disease can be transmitted to humans through eating meat from infected cattle, there is really no reason why people should avoid eating beef. The sale of all animal feed that contains other animal products has been prohibited.

53. Which of the following pieces of information is needed to make the above argument reasonable?

    (1) the total number of human deaths from BSE worldwide
    (2) the number of cattle given only plant feed
    (3) how much beef the average American eats
    (4) the measures taken to identify cattle infected before the feed ban
    (5) the number of deaths from Legionnaire's disease

Typical Function of Some Endocrine Glands

Gland	Activity Regulated
Pituitary	growth; regulates other glands
Thyroid	metabolic rate (body weight)
Thymus	lymphatic system (immunity)
Parathyroid	calcium metabolism (nervous system)
Pancreas	insulin production (sugar metabolism)
Adrenal cortex	salt & carbohydrate metabolism

54. Diabetes is caused by the insufficient production of insulin. Based on the above table, a malfunction in which of the body's endocrine glands might lead to diabetes?

    (1) adrenal cortex
    (2) thyroid gland
    (3) pancreas
    (4) parathyroid
    (5) thymus

Some scientists believe that, to some extent, an animal's life span is predetermined. The free radical theory of aging states that as a body grows older, its cells produce chemicals called free radicals, which eventually destroy the body's cells. The programmed senescence theory of aging states that the death of cells is controlled by an animal's genes.

55. If both of these theories prove to be correct and to work in unison, which of the following conclusions can be drawn?

    (1) Free radicals can be eliminated from the body to give it longer life.
    (2) Genes have little or no effect on free radicals.
    (3) The production of free radicals is controlled by genes.
    (4) Death can be overcome with cloning.
    (5) Certain vitamins prevent the formation of free radicals.

Questions 56 through 58 refer to the following passage.

Bacteria are helpful in the breakdown of dead organisms into simple molecules that can then be reused by new organisms. Some bacteria that live in nodules on the roots of plants in the pea family help replenish the soil with nitrogen essential for plant growth. People use bacteria which cause fermentation to preserve foods such as cheese, vinegar, and sauerkraut for human consumption and silage for cattle. Bacteria are also used in sewage treatment plants to purify water and in pharmaceutical laboratories to produce insulin for diabetics.

Other bacteria are considered harmful. Some cause food spoilage and poisoning, as in botulism and salmonellosis. Both plants and animals can become diseased by the invasion of certain bacteria. Leprosy, diphtheria, tuberculosis, gonorrhea, typhoid fever, and pneumonia are all bacterial infections affecting people. Black rot in cabbages and anthrax in sheep are also diseases caused by bacteria.

56. Which of the following statements best summarizes the information presented about bacteria?

    (1) Bacteria are never harmful and are essential to human life.
    (2) All bacteria are harmful.
    (3) Both plants and animals can be harmed by bacteria.
    (4) Some bacteria are harmful to humans, but others are helpful.
    (5) Bacteria are more beneficial than harmful.

57. According to the passage, how are some bacteria helpful to humans?

    By

    (1) killing the organism that causes cabbage rot
    (2) producing insulin needed by diabetics
    (3) purifying foods contaminated by salmonella
    (4) curing anthrax in sheep
    (5) poisoning the harmful members of the pea family

58. Which relationship is similar to that of bacteria to pneumonia?

    (1) cigarettes to lung cancer
    (2) viruses to bacteria
    (3) diarrhea to intestinal parasites
    (4) salmonella bacteria to food
    (5) accidents to death

Question 59 refers to the following illustration.

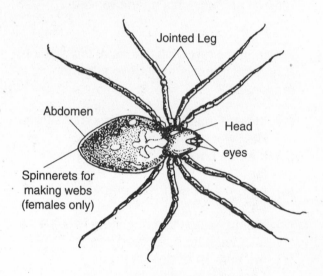

59. All insects have six legs and three body sections called the head, thorax, and abdomen. Why is the spider in the diagram not an insect?

    Because it has

    (1) eyes on top of its head
    (2) legs facing forward
    (3) pairs of legs each having three jointed sections
    (4) an abdomen bigger than its head
    (5) eight legs and two body sections

Question 60 refers to the following paragraph.

Inherited genes determine what an individual may become; environment determines what an individual will become. A person may inherit musical ability from ancestors, but whether the person will be a musician is decided by factors in the environment.

60. According to the passage, which of the following statements describes the ability of an individual to excel at sports?

The ability to excel

(1) has no limits
(2) is only a result of inheritance
(3) is only a result of what a person eats
(4) is limited by inheritance but influenced by environmental factors
(5) will significantly increase with exercise

Questions 61 and 62 refer to the following paragraph.

An advertisement for drinkable fiber says the drink includes the grain psyllium because the grain contains soluble fiber. Fiber assists in retaining sufficient water in the lower intestine to keep stools soft. This then helps a person maintain regular and comfortable bowel movements.

61. Which of the following questions would be unimportant in determining whether to use the advertised product?

(1) Does the individual need to include more fiber in the diet?
(2) Can the individual's diet be adjusted to include sufficient fiber from foods?
(3) Is psyllium grown by regular farming methods?
(4) If psyllium contains soluble fiber, does it hold as much water as insoluble fibers?
(5) Are any side effects caused by using this grain?

62. In the U.S. more money is spent on purgatives (medicine promoting evacuation of the bowels) than any other over-the-counter medicine. Many of the purchasers are elderly people who frequently experience irregularity. Which of the following factors is unlikely to contribute to this problem?

(1) lack of sufficient exercise to stimulate the movement of food through the body
(2) lack of sufficient money to purchase high fiber fruits, vegetables, and grains
(3) breakdown of body processes so that the body does not function as well
(4) inability to know that a problem exists
(5) lack of interest in eating full regular meals that include a variety of food

---

Questions 63 and 64 refer to the following paragraph.

At a health convention, a natural food salesperson warns, "Chemicals are the cause of cancer. If people would just buy natural foods instead of chemicals, our society would rid itself of this disease."

63. Not knowing that chemicals are the basic ingredients of all matter identifies the speaker as which of the following?

(1) overeducated
(2) interesting
(3) misinformed
(4) unintelligent
(5) literate

64. What is the basic fallacy (false assumption) in the sales pitch?

(1) Chemicals do not cause cancer.
(2) Chemicals are always safe.
(3) Natural substances are not chemicals.
(4) Chemicals changed by humans are safe.
(5) Chemicals are sometimes produced in laboratories.

65. Oxygen is an odorless, colorless gas essential to life. In which of the following places is oxygen most likely to be found supporting life?

(1) deep sea vent
(2) topsoil
(3) volcanic hot springs
(4) stratosphere
(5) metal ore

Questions 66 through 71 refer to the following information.

A large variety of organisms live on the continental shelves, which are covered with ocean water. The most numerous organisms are the floating plankton. Zooplankton are microscopic animals, and phytoplankton are microscopic plants. Phytoplankton contain green chloroplasts and live near the surface of the ocean in order to receive enough light to synthesize their own food from carbon dioxide (CO_2) and water. Zooplankton have no green chloroplasts, cannot make their own food, and must eat phytoplankton. Fish and other swimming sea animals, called nekton, constantly supply carbon dioxide which the phytoplankton must have to synthesize food.

Nekton eat plankton and other nekton. Benthos crawl on the sea floor, eating waste materials and dead plants and animals that have sunk to the bottom.

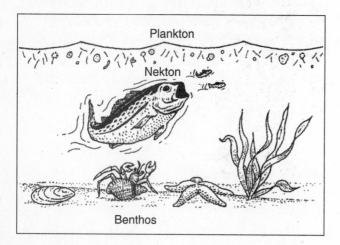

66. The ocean floor (benthos region) would be the natural home for which of the following sea organisms?

    (1) dolphins
    (2) whales
    (3) plankton
    (4) shrimp
    (5) swordfish

67. If the phytoplankton in the ocean were to die off, which ocean animals would be affected?

    (1) none
    (2) zooplankton only
    (3) nekton only
    (4) benthos organisms only
    (5) all ocean animals

68. In brown or red seaweed, the green chlorophyll is hidden by other chemicals. Giant kelp, a brown seaweed, often grows to 200 feet in length. Kelp has air bladders to help it float. What is the most likely reason this seaweed floats?

    To

    (1) trap phytoplankton
    (2) trap lobsters and fish
    (3) help kelp swim
    (4) keep kelp near the sunlight
    (5) help kelp stay near the air for easy breathing

69. Nekton are active swimmers that occupy specific levels within the ocean. A fish's color depends on the level to which that species has adapted. Saltwater surface fish are usually blue or gray, mid-level fish are whitish or silvery, and very deep fish are very dark colors. A shopper observes a fish at a fish counter. The fish's skin is dark brown. Which of the following is probably true of the this fish?

    It

    (1) eats plankton
    (2) is a freshwater river fish
    (3) is a deep-water fish
    (4) is not a true fish but a type of squid
    (5) is best served with butter

70. Who would be the most likely people to be interested in the specific levels occupied by different fish species?

    (1) beach surfers
    (2) fishers
    (3) navigators of military ships
    (4) captains of ocean cruisers
    (5) Caribbean tourists

71. Many of the sun's rays are reflected off the ocean surface. The rays that enter the ocean water are absorbed by the water as thermal energy. Little light penetrates deep ocean water. Which statement below is most likely?

    (1) Deep water is hotter than surface water.
    (2) Phytoplankton need little light energy.
    (3) It is not very dark in deep ocean water.
    (4) Deep-water fish are adapted to warm tempratures.
    (5) Deep-water fish are often blind or have no eyes.

UNIT 2 Earth and Space Science

Directions: Choose the one best answer to each question.

Question 1 refers to the following information.

Chlorofluorocarbons (CFCs) and related chemicals are human-made substances primarily used in air conditioning and refrigeration. They are known to destroy the layer of ozone in the atmosphere that protects Earth from harmful ultraviolet (UV) rays from the sun. The table below shows the ozone-depleting potential (ODP) for various substances. CFC-11 is used as a base for comparison, and it has been assigned an ODP of 1. Other ODP numbers indicate a substance's damaging effects on the ozone layer as compared with CFC-11.

Ozone Depleting Potential (ODP) of Selected Substances		
Group	Substance	ODP
CFC's	CFC-11	1.0
	CFC-13	0.8
	CFC-14	1.0
Halons	Halon 1211	3.0
	Halon 1301	10.0
Carbon Tetrachloride	CC14	1.1

1. If you wanted to buy an air conditioner that contained the least damaging refrigerant, which of the following would you choose?

   (1) CFC-13
   (2) CFC-14
   (3) Halon 1211
   (4) Halon 1301
   (5) CC 14

Question 2 refers to the following passage.

The majority of tornadoes develop from severe thunderstorms. There must be a layer of warm, moist air near the ground, with a layer of much cooler air above it. The warm air rises but stops at higher elevations and spreads sideways to form a large, anvil-shaped thundercloud. In addition, the winds at higher elevations must differ substantially in speed, direction, or both from those at lower elevations, which creates a wind shear. The wind shear causes the rising air to swirl, producing a rotating column of air. A dark wall cloud forms underneath this rotating column of air. Twisting tornado funnels that rotate counterclockwise develop out of the wall cloud and descend to the ground. The first signs of an impending tornado are often rain followed by hail. When the hail stops, a tornado may hit.

2. Based on the passage, which of the following may aid in tornado formation?

   (1) winds at higher elevations the same as those at lower elevations
   (2) a layer of cool air near the ground with a layer of warm, moist air above
   (3) a wall cloud beneath a thundercloud
   (4) hail and rain
   (5) winds blowing clockwise

3. In 1994 the U.S. launched the Geostationary Operational Environmental Satellite (GOES). GOES is one of two weather satellites that produces images of clouds and measures cloud heights. These data are used in three-dimensional models of the weather.

   The data gathered by GOES are most useful for which of the following?

   (1) tracking acid rain pollution
   (2) analyzing traffic patterns
   (3) detecting variations in ocean currents
   (4) forecasting storms
   (5) detecting wildfires

Question 4 refers to the following information.

In some developing countries, forests—especially rain forests—are rapidly disappearing because of people's reliance on wood. The graph below shows the ways in which wood was used in developing countries in the year 1995. Most wood was used by individuals and families for heat or cooking fuel (in the form of the wood itself or as charcoal). Some wood was used by industry and for paper products.

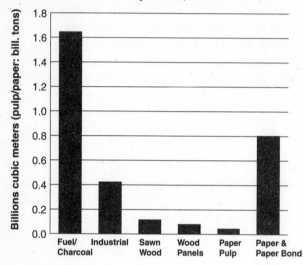

Forest Products Produced in Developing Countries, by Volume, 1995

4. Based on the graph, which of the following alternatives would do the most to save forests in developing countries?

   (1) building dams for hydroelectric power for industry
   (2) providing solar-powered cookers and heaters for homes
   (3) using recycled paper products in industry and government
   (4) building homes made of concrete blocks
   (5) forbidding use of wood paneling in the U.S.

Question 5 refers to the following map.

Eruption of Mount St. Helens

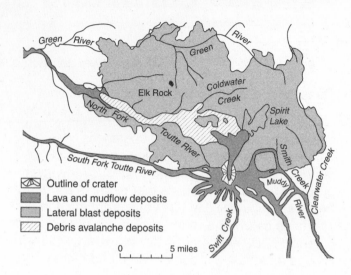

Legend:
- Outline of crater
- Lava and mudflow deposits
- Lateral blast deposits
- Debris avalanche deposits

0 — 5 miles

The map above shows the immediate effects of the eruption of Mount St. Helens volcano in 1980. A large area of forest surrounding the volcano was flattened and covered with blast deposits, or ash. Surrounding rivers flowed with lava and burning hot mud.

5. Based on the map, which of the following effects of the erruption had on impact on areas farthest from the volcano itself?

   (1) lateral blast deposits (ash)
   (2) crater collapse
   (3) lava and mudflow deposits
   (4) floods
   (5) debris avalanche deposits (rock and soil)

Questions 6 through 10 refer to the following illustration.

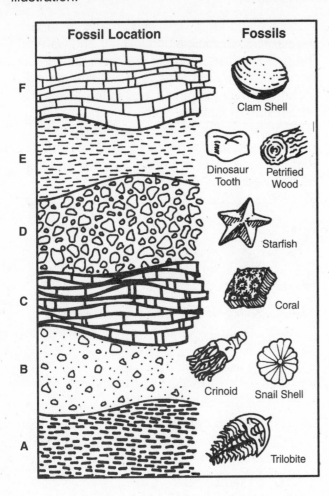

Fossil Location | Fossils

F

Clam Shell

E

Dinosaur Tooth   Petrified Wood

D

Starfish

C

Coral

B

Crinoid   Snail Shell

A

Trilobite

6. The law of superposition states that, for sedimentary rock, the layer below is always older. From the illustration, what can one assume is the oldest fossil pictured?

(1) clam
(2) coral
(3) crinoid
(4) snail
(5) trilobite

7. Based on the illustration, what is apparent about fossils?

That they are usually from

(1) plants
(2) extinct animals
(3) freshwater organisms
(4) land organisms
(5) hard parts of plants and animals

8. From the fossils imbedded in rock layer C, what can one conclude about the likely development of that layer?

It developed

(1) from a river bed
(2) on the ocean floor
(3) in a desert
(4) on forested land
(5) on a sheer mountain peak

9. Which of the following statements is contradicted by the fossil evidence in the illustration?

(1) Bivalves such as clams evolved from snails.
(2) Trilobites lived many millions of years ago.
(3) Starfish evolved from crinoids.
(4) Crinoids and snails first appeared in the oceans about the same time.
(5) Clams were the first kind of animal to evolve in the oceans.

10. If a scientist found the fossils shown in the illustration by digging down at one spot, what could he or she infer about the geological history of that spot?

(1) It was covered by the sea for a long time, then became dry land, then was covered by the sea again.
(2) It was always covered by the sea, until recent times.
(3) It was always dry land.
(4) It was part of a continent that drifted north from the South Pole.
(5) It has been covered by the sea for only a short time.

Questions 11 and 12 refer to the following illustration.

A maritime air mass refers to air that has spent time over a sea or ocean, while a continental air mass refers to air that has spent time over land.

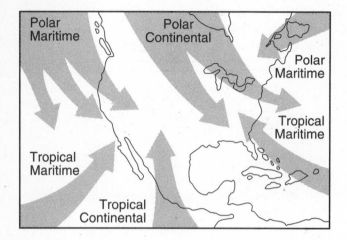

11. An air mass moving south from central Canada toward the midwest section of the United States would most likely be which of the following?

    (1) wet and cool
    (2) wet and fast
    (3) humid and frigid
    (4) dry and cool
    (5) dry and hot

12. The hotter the air, the faster ocean water evaporates. Hurricanes develop near the equator when spinning air, holding large quantities of water, accelerates to speeds over 70 miles per hour. In which of the following air masses do most hurricanes form?

    (1) polar continental
    (2) polar maritime
    (3) tropical maritime
    (4) tropical continental
    (5) all types of air masses

Questions 13 through 15 refer to the following information.

Soil is made up of decaying organic material and particles of rock, along with air and water. The rock particles range in size from almost-microscopic clay particles to gravel-size chunks. These components of soil tend to form layers. A certain kind of material dominates each layer.

The upper layers of soil contain most of the nutrients required for plant growth. They come from the soil's decaying organic matter and from the minerals in the soil's rock particles.

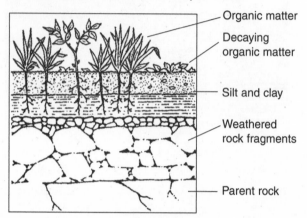

13. Earthworms eat decaying plant material in soil. Where would you expect to find the greatest number of earthworms?

    (1) on the surface
    (2) in the uppermost layer of soil
    (3) in the layer of silt and clay
    (4) in the layer of weathered rock
    (5) in the layer of parent rock

14. Of the following places, where would you probably find the deepest soil?

    (1) in a desert
    (2) on a mountainside
    (3) near the Arctic circle
    (4) in a forest
    (5) in the parent rock below

15. Which of the following soils is probably best for growing crops?

    (1) soil with a thick organic layer and no silt and clay
    (2) soil with thick layers of organic material and silt and clay
    (3) soil with no organic layer
    (4) soil with thin layers of organic material and silt and clay
    (5) soil with a thin organic layer and a hard-packed silt and clay layer

Questions 16 and 17 refer to the following paragraphs.

Water and wind transport sand. In time, sand may form a sedimentary rock called sandstone.

Limestone is another kind of sedimentary rock. Some kinds of limestone form when layers of sediments containing the shells and skeletons of dead sea organisms pile up on the ocean floor.

16. If a geologist digs down into rock in Indiana and finds a layer of limestone, what can the geologist conclude?

    (1) Indiana was once covered by an ocean.
    (2) Indiana was once a desert.
    (3) A giant tidal wave must have sent water to the center of the United States.
    (4) An underground ocean once existed in that area.
    (5) Fish and sea creatures once lived on land.

17. Sedimentary rocks form in horizontal layers, like a sandwich. If you found sandstone in which each layer was a different color, this would be evidence of which of the following?

    (1) The sand that formed the rock came from the ocean.
    (2) A geological process sorted the sand by color before it became rock.
    (3) Animals burrowed in the sand before it became rock.
    (4) The sand that formed the rock was blown there from different places.
    (5) The sandstone was quarried in a certain way.

18. Sandstone blocks can be cut and used instead of bricks for constructing buildings. Houses made of sandstone are often called brownstone houses. Sandstone is unusually absorbent but neither rusts like metals nor rots like wood. However, smoke and dirt cling to sandstone and give it a dingy appearance. Which is the most likely way brownstone houses are given a fresh, clean look?

    By

    (1) painting with spray guns
    (2) washing with cleaning fluid
    (3) sandblasting with air guns
    (4) varnishing with hand brushes
    (5) covering with wallpaper

19. Limestone (a rock) and clay (a soil) are mixed, then baked, and later ground to form cement. Cement is usually mixed with sand and gravel to make concrete. Limestone, soda ash, and sand are mixed, then heated, and molded or formed into glass objects. Modern societies use tremendous amounts of cement and glass for structures and objects of value. Which of the following structures or objects is made without limestone rock?

    (1) masonry blocks
    (2) glass bottles
    (3) windowpanes
    (4) sidewalks
    (5) plastic

20. Some scientists believe that pollution in the atmosphere is causing the average temperature of Earth's surface to increase and that it will continue to increase over a period of many years. They call this trend global warming. Which of the following provides the most convincing evidence for global warming?

    (1) an unusually warm summer in Indiana
    (2) two winters in a row in Norway with unusually warm temperatures
    (3) a three-inch rise in the level of the oceans over several decades caused by partial melting of the polar ice caps
    (4) a heat wave that breaks high-temperature records across much of the United States
    (5) average temperatures 1 to 3 degrees higher than last year's tempratures in five European cities

Question 21 refers to the following information.

Beautiful minerals from rocks are sometimes worn as jewelry. Minerals called gems are usually quite scarce, which makes them valuable. Beautiful minerals that are plentiful are called semiprecious stones. The color of semiprecious stones or gems depends on the minerals and impurities they contain. Expensive jewelry often uses bright, colorful stones.

21. Why are rubies red, sapphires blue, and emeralds green?

Because they

(1) are scarce
(2) are valuable
(3) are found in rocks that are very hard
(4) contain different minerals and impurities
(5) are gems and not semiprecious stones

Questions 22 through 24 refer to the following information.

At sea level, the weight of air exerts 14.7 pounds of pressure on each square inch of Earth's surface. At any point above sea level, there are fewer air molecules in the column of air pressing down on Earth. Thus, air pressure decreases at surfaces above sea level.

22. What could an instrument that measures air pressure very precisely be used to determine?

(1) temperature
(2) latitude
(3) elevation
(4) humidity
(5) wind speed

23. What can you conclude from the drawing below?

(1) The pressure of the atmospheric air decreases as elevation decreases.
(2) The pressure of the atmospheric air increases as the elevation decreases.
(3) The amount of air inside the balloon increases as the elevation decreases.
(4) The amount of air inside the balloon decreases as the elevation decreases.
(5) The changing volume of the balloon is independent of the atmospheric pressure.

Air Pressure and Balloon Size

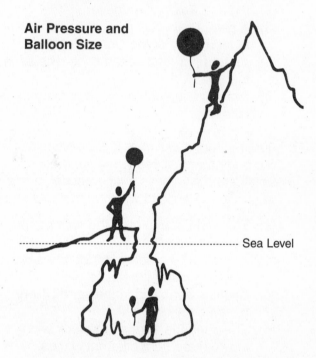

Sea Level

24. Which of the following examples illustrates the same principle as the drawing?

(1) Yeast breads at lower elevations rise faster and higher than those at high elevations.
(2) Deep sea divers must wear pressurized suits to maintain breathing and to prevent eardrums from bursting inward.
(3) Astronauts walking in space or on the moon weigh less than they do on Earth.
(4) Mountain climers need supplemental oxygen at high elevations.
(5) Trees are unable to grow on high mountain tops where air pressure is decreased.

25. Ores are rocks that contain one or more metals. Copper and iron are both metals. From this information what can one deduce?

(1) Copper and iron are strong.
(2) Iron is heavier than copper.
(3) Copper and iron come from rock materials.
(4) Copper and iron are valuable.
(5) Copper and iron are obtained from the same ore.

Question 26 refers to the following information.

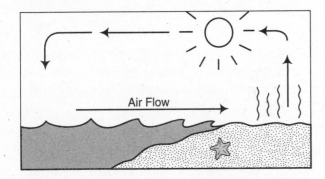

Air Flow

26. When air is hot, it rises. When air is cooled, it sinks, which causes wind. Which of the following conditions exist at sea coasts?

(1) The sand is cooler than the water.
(2) During the daytime, a warm breeze moves inland off the water.
(3) The water temperature is higher than the temperature of the sand.
(4) The sun sends more rays to land than it does to water.
(5) The water cools the air above it, causing the air to sink.

Questions 27 through 29 refer to the following information.

Average Yearly Earthquakes for Selected States

States	Earthquakes	High Intensity Quakes
Alaska	266	8
Arizona	24	1
California	830	30
Colorado	59	0
Hawaii	121	3
Montana	150	7
North Dakota	0	0
New York	52	2
Utah	101	3
Washington	141	10
West Virginia	6	0

27. Which of the statements below can be supported by data in the table?

A. Earthquakes do not happen on the East Coast.
B. Islands have almost no earthquake risk.
C. California has the greatest number of earthquakes.
D. None of Colorado's earthquakes were of high intensity.

(1) A only
(2) A and B
(3) A and C
(4) C and D
(5) B, C, and D

28. Which of the following states has the greatest proportion of high-intensity quakes to the total number of earthquakes?

(1) California
(2) Colorado
(3) North Dakota
(4) Utah
(5) Washington

29. The greatest number of earthquakes occur in which states?

Those states

(1) in, near, or bordering the Pacific Ocean
(2) in, near, or bordering the Atlantic Ocean
(3) bordering Mexico or the Gulf of Mexico
(4) surrounding the Great Lakes
(5) in the central U.S. Great Plains

Question 30 refers to the following table.

The table below shows the relative hardness of some common minerals and objects.

Scale of Rock Hardness			
	Relative Hardness Number	Mineral/Rock	Common Objects
HARDEST	10	Diamond	
	8	Topaz	
	7	Quartz	
	6	Potassium feldspar (iron)	
			pocket knife glass
	5	Apatite	
	4	Fluorite	
			pennies
	3	Calcite	
			fingernails
	2	Gypsum	
SOFTEST	1	Talc	

30. If you wanted to etch a design into a glass window, which of the following materials would do the best etching job?

(1) gypsum block
(2) topaz ring
(3) mineral calcite
(4) copper needle
(5) pocket knife

Question 31 refers to the following information.

Between 1987 and 1997, development—that is, building homes and shopping malls—consumed about 23 million acres of land in the U.S. At the same time, forest land declined about 3 million acres, pasture land about 9 million acres, and cropland about 32 million acres.

31. Based on this information, which of the following land types most needs protection?

(1) forest
(2) suburban
(3) range
(4) crop
(5) developed

Question 32 refers to the following information.

Mountain ranges are often formed when two continental plates collide. At the place where two plates crash into each other, land is crumpled and forced upward to form mountain ranges.

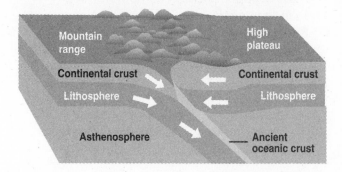

32. Based on the above diagram showing the collision of two continental plates, the mountain ranges are being created from which of the following?

(1) high plateau
(2) continental crust
(3) lithosphere
(4) asthenosphere
(5) ancient oceanic crust

33. Air bubbles trapped in ice contain the precise mix of gases in the atmosphere at the time the ice was formed. Scientists have analyzed samples of ice from places such as Antarctica and Greenland to study the composition of the atmosphere as it was long ago. The scientists have used these data to determine if the current increase in greenhouse gases is a natural phenomenon or is a result of human activity.

Which of the following methods of scientific analysis are the scientists using in the above study?

(1) controlled laboratory experiments
(2) on-site measurements of greenhouse gases
(3) comparing data over time
(4) trial and error
(5) reproducing previous experiments

Question 34 refers to the following graph.

The graph below indicates that when a streamside forest is clearcut, rain falling on the cleared land runs off at a much greater rate. The increased runoff into the stream causes the stream height (its height above sea level) to rise. The graph also shows that as plants grow again on the clearcut land, runoff and stream height decline, and eventually return to normal.

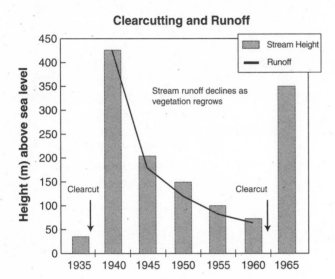

Clearcutting and Runoff

34. Based on the graph, which of the following conclusions can be made?

   (1) Rain washes vegetation into streams.
   (2) Clearcutting improves fish habitats by adding water to streams.
   (3) Vegetation on land absorbs a lot of rain water, thus limiting runoff.
   (4) Streams never recover after forests are clearcut.
   (5) Streams can absorb unlimited amounts of soil and can rise indefinitely.

Question 35 refers to the following information.

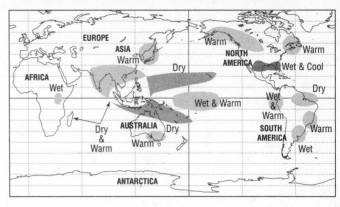

El Niño is a weather phenomenon caused by an unusual warming of the tropical Pacific Ocean. During an El Niño, climate patterns around the world are disrupted, and unusual weather occurs in many parts of the globe. For example, between December and February, parts of Asia and Australia that would normally get lots of rain get very little or no precipitation. The map above shows El Niño weather patterns.

35. If you knew that an El Niño was developing, which of the following weather patterns would you expect to hear about in the United States?

   (1) hotter, drier summers in the Northeast
   (2) a winter drought in the Southwest
   (3) cold, wet weather in Alaska
   (4) cooler and wetter winter weather in the Southeast
   (5) hotter and wetter summer weather in the West

36. Erosion occurs when rocks or soil are moved from one place and deposited in another place. An agent of erosion is a force that has the energy to cause rocks or soil to move. Which of the following agents of erosion is the greatest factor in moving tropical desert sands and soils into piles called dunes?

   (1) running water
   (2) wind
   (3) gravity
   (4) ocean waves
   (5) glaciers

37. Salt is a mineral found in certain rocks and soils. Most table salt is obtained from inland underground mines. Salt is also abundant in oceans. What is the most likely reason salt is found in oceans?

Salt

(1) occurs only in rocks found at the bottom of oceans
(2) evaporates from rocks into the air
(3) dissolves in rainwater and is carried by rivers to the oceans
(4) is formed into rocks by animals in the oceans
(5) is a waste product dumped into the oceans by humans

Question 38 refers to the following drawing.

EARTH'S REVOLUTION AROUND THE SUN

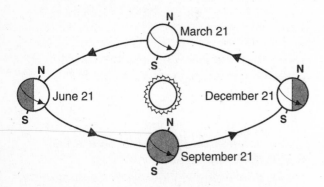

38. In the Northern Hemisphere, what is the date having the longest day and shortest night?

(1) January 21
(2) March 21
(3) June 21
(4) November 21
(5) December 21

Questions 39 and 40 refer to the following information.

Operating the devices used by people today requires substantial amounts of energy. Some of the ways people obtain this energy are listed below.

solar collection—using cells that collect heat from sunlight

burning fuels—obtaining heat from the remains of living material (wood, coal, petroleum, or natural gas)

nuclear fission—breaking apart certain atoms to release energy

geothermal energy—obtaining heat by digging deep into Earth's crust

tidal energy—using the natural movements of ocean water to operate turbines to generate electricity

39. Which of the methods described is currently used to operate most land and air vehicles?

(1) solar cells
(2) burning fuels
(3) nuclear fission
(4) geothermal energy
(5) tidal energy

40. Which of the following sources of energy is most in danger of becoming exhausted?

(1) solar energy
(2) fossil fuels
(3) nuclear energy
(4) geothermal energy
(5) tidal energy

Questions 41 through 43 refer to the following information.

When Earth makes one complete rotation on its axis, one day has passed. A year is measured by one revolution of Earth around the sun. During one year, 365 days, 5 hours, 48 minutes, and 46 seconds pass. To account for the extra hours and minutes, an extra day, February 29, is added every fourth year and on years ending in 00 and divisible by 400.

To make a calendar, one must account for the need of 365 days on regular years and 366 days on leap years. In 1931, the League of Nations held an international conference on calendar reform. One of the more than 500 plans submitted that was seriously considered for worldwide usage was the thirteen-month calendar below. Agreement could not be reached on any one calendar; thus still today, many different calendars are used throughout the world.

The Thirteen-Month Calendar

JANUARY
S	M	T	W	T	F	S
1	2	3	4	5	6	7
8	9	10	11	12	13	14
15	16	17	18	19	20	21
22	23	24	25	26	27	28

FEBRUARY
S	M	T	W	T	F	S
1	2	3	4	5	6	7
8	9	10	11	12	13	14
15	16	17	18	19	20	21
22	23	24	25	26	27	28

MARCH
S	M	T	W	T	F	S
1	2	3	4	5	6	7
8	9	10	11	12	13	14
15	16	17	18	19	20	21
22	23	24	25	26	27	28

APRIL
S	M	T	W	T	F	S
1	2	3	4	5	6	7
8	9	10	11	12	13	14
15	16	17	18	19	20	21
22	23	24	25	26	27	28

MAY
S	M	T	W	T	F	S
1	2	3	4	5	6	7
8	9	10	11	12	13	14
15	16	17	18	19	20	21
22	23	24	25	26	27	28

JUNE
S	M	T	W	T	F	S
1	2	3	4	5	6	7
8	9	10	11	12	13	14
15	16	17	18	19	20	21
22	23	24	25	26	27	28

LEAP DAY
June 29

SOL
S	M	T	W	T	F	S
1	2	3	4	5	6	7
8	9	10	11	12	13	14
15	16	17	18	19	20	21
22	23	24	25	26	27	28

JULY
S	M	T	W	T	F	S
1	2	3	4	5	6	7
8	9	10	11	12	13	14
15	16	17	18	19	20	21
22	23	24	25	26	27	28

AUGUST
S	M	T	W	T	F	S
1	2	3	4	5	6	7
8	9	10	11	12	13	14
15	16	17	18	19	20	21
22	23	24	25	26	27	28

SEPTEMBER
S	M	T	W	T	F	S
1	2	3	4	5	6	7
8	9	10	11	12	13	14
15	16	17	18	19	20	21
22	23	24	25	26	27	28

OCTOBER
S	M	T	W	T	F	S
1	2	3	4	5	6	7
8	9	10	11	12	13	14
15	16	17	18	19	20	21
22	23	24	25	26	27	28

NOVEMBER
S	M	T	W	T	F	S
1	2	3	4	5	6	7
8	9	10	11	12	13	14
15	16	17	18	19	20	21
22	23	24	25	26	27	28

DECEMBER
S	M	T	W	T	F	S
1	2	3	4	5	6	7
8	9	10	11	12	13	14
15	16	17	18	19	20	21
22	23	24	25	26	27	28

YEAR DAY
December 29

41. Which of the following features is a characteristic of the thirteen-month calendar?

   (1) The thirteenth month appears only in leap year.
   (2) All years have the same number of days.
   (3) Each year a person's birthday would fall on the same day of the week.
   (4) Every month would always begin on a Saturday.
   (5) There would be no leap year day.

42. Which of the following is determined by the movements of Earth in relation to the sun, and not by social convention?

   (1) length of a week
   (2) when the year begins
   (3) number of weekends in a year
   (4) length of a year
   (5) the day on which Thanksgiving falls

43. In the thirteen-month calendar, why is a "year day" needed every year?

   (1) to celebrate a special holiday on the last day of the year
   (2) because a year is a few hours more than 365 days long
   (3) to celebrate the birthday of the inventor of the calendar
   (4) because 365 divided by 13 has a remainder of 1
   (5) because 13 is an odd number

Directions: Choose the <u>one best answer</u> to each question.

<u>Question 1</u> refers to the following illustration.

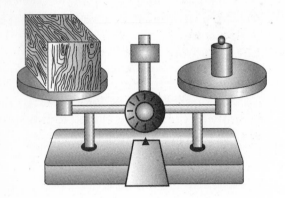

1. The scale is in balance, so the two objects shown on the scale have the same mass. Yet one object is much smaller than the other. Which of the following must be true regarding the smaller object?

   (1) It is harder than the larger object.
   (2) It weighs more than the larger object.
   (3) It has a greater density than the larger object.
   (4) It has a lower center of gravity than the larger object.
   (5) It has more inertia than the larger object.

2. A common chemical reaction is corrosion, which usually occurs when certain metals react with their environment in the presence of water and oxygen. The following equation describes the corrosion of iron, which is called rusting.

   $$4Fe(OH)_2 + O_2 ----- > 2(Fe_2O_3 + 2H_2O)$$

   Which of the following terms describes corrosion?

   (1) polymerization
   (2) oxidation
   (3) fermentation
   (4) evaporation
   (5) convection

<u>Question 3</u> refers to the following information.

A colloid is a mixture in which clusters of molecules of one substance are permanently dispersed throughout another substance. The substances in a colloid do not separate, even if the mixture is passed through a paper filter. Milk, for example, is a colloid in which particles of proteins, fats, and sugars are permanently suspended.

Types and Examples of Colloids

Name	Nature	Example
foam	gas dispersed in liquid	whipped cream
solid foam	gas dispersed in solid	marshmallow
liquid aerosol	liquid dispersed in gas	mist
sol	solid dispersed in liquid	jelly
solid aerosol	solid dispersed in gas	smoke
emulsion	liquid dispersed in liquid	mayonnaise
solid emulsion	liquid dispersed in solid	butter

3. The above table describes various kinds of colloids and lists examples. Based on the information in the table, which of the following is also a colloid?

   (1) carbonated soda
   (2) shaving cream
   (3) muddy water
   (4) soap bubbles in bath water
   (5) air in a balloon

Question 4 refers to the following table.

Chemical Formulas for Some Organic Substances

Beet Sugar	$C_{12}H_{22}O_{11}$
Grain Alcohol	C_2H_5OH
Methane	CH_4
Propane	C_3H_8
Ether	$CH_3OCH_2CH_3$
Alanine (amino acid)	$CH_3CH(NH_2)COOH$

C = Carbon	**H** = Hydrogen
O = Oxygen	**N** = Nitrogen

4. Based on the formulas in the table, which of the following combinations of elements do all organic compounds have in common?

   (1) carbon and nitrogen
   (2) hydrogen and carbon
   (3) hydrogen and oxygen
   (4) oxygen and carbon
   (5) carbon, hydrogen, and oxygen

Question 5 refers to the following passage.

In the early 1800s, chemist Amedeo Avogadro studied the molecular composition of gases. What he learned has become a universal law of chemistry. Avogadro's law states that under identical conditions of temperature and pressure, equal volumes of gases contain an equal number of molecules.

5. Two identical bottles, one filled with helium and one filled with oxygen, are placed under the same conditions of temperature and pressure. According to Avogadro's Law, which of the following must be true?

   (1) There are more helium molecules than oxygen molecules.
   (2) There are more oxygen molecules than helium molecules.
   (3) There are the same number of helium and oxygen molecules.
   (4) There are more helium atoms than oxygen atoms.
   (5) There is the same number of helium and oxygen atoms.

Question 6 refers to the following passage.

In 1989, scientists announced that they had successfully achieved "cold fusion." Fusion is the uniting of atomic nuclei, an energy-producing process that occurs in the sun at extremely high temperatures. If what the researchers claimed was true—that fusion of hydrogen nuclei could take place at low temperatures—then the world would have an unlimited and completely clean source of energy.

Unfortunately, after announcing their research results, the scientists were questioned about their methods and their claims. Other scientists were unable to get the same results when they reproduced the original fusion experiment. Shortly thereafter, physicists determined that the original research had been flawed.

6. The claim that cold fusion had been achieved was dismissed because the science that led to it violated which of the following conventions of scientific inquiry?

   (1) Experiments must be carefully observed.
   (2) The original hypothesis must be correct.
   (3) Data must be gathered and interpreted.
   (4) Experiments and results must be reproducible.
   (5) Hydrogen nuclei fuse only at temperatures of millions of degrees.

Questions 7 through 10 refer to the following chart.

Approximate Densities* of Some Seasoned (Cured) Wood	
Pine	0.35–0.6 cm^3
Cedar	0.3–0.4 cm^3
Spruce	0.5–0.7 cm^3
Hickory, maple, oak	0.6–0.9 cm^3
Walnut	0.7 cm^3
Ebony	1.2 cm^3

* Grams per cubic centimeters

7. The density of all objects is compared to the density of water, which is 1.0 gm/cm^3. Objects with densities less than 1 gm/cm^3 will float, and those with densities greater than 1 gm/cm^3 will sink in water. Which of the following woods will sink in water?

    (1) ebony only
    (2) ebony and walnut
    (3) hickory, maple, and oak
    (4) pine only
    (5) all woods

8. Hardwoods have high densities and softwoods have low densities. Cutting and nailing hardwoods is more difficult, but softwoods dent and scratch more easily. Which person would most likely need the information provided by the table?

    (1) carpenter
    (2) apartment supervisor
    (3) road contractor
    (4) welder
    (5) interior designer

9. When would the information in the table be most important?

    When purchasing wood by the

    (1) pound
    (2) tree
    (3) board foot
    (4) truckload
    (5) wood type

10. Pine and cedar are considered softwoods. Hickory, maple, oak, and walnut are considered hardwoods. Based on this information and the densities listed in the table, how is hardwood best defined?

    As a wood with a density

    (1) greater than 0.4 gm/cm^3
    (2) greater than 0.5 gm/cm^3
    (3) of 0.6 gm/cm^3 or greater
    (4) of 0.7 gm/cm^3 or greater
    (5) between 0.6 gm/cm^3 and 0.9 gm/cm^3

11. Despite the fact that many gases are invisible, odorless, and colorless, gases do occupy space, have weight, and are thus matter. Which of the following statements supports the fact that Earth's atmosphere contains matter?

    (1) Heat shield tiles get hot during the re-entry of the space shuttle craft.
    (2) People find it difficult to breathe at high elevations.
    (3) Animals have evolved different means of breathing.
    (4) Humans have walked on the moon and found no atmosphere there.
    (5) Airplanes can fly in outer space but not in the troposphere.

Question 12 refers to the following diagram.

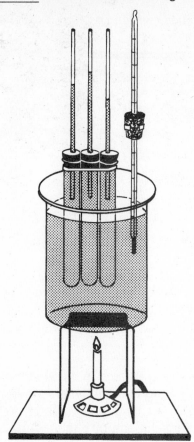

Thermal Expansion of Heated Liquids

12. Observation of the diagram above supports which of the following conclusions?

    (1) Heat does not affect temperature.
    (2) The temperature of the heated liquid is being measured.
    (3) The three test tubes each contain different liquids.
    (4) The liquids in the test tubes have contracted in volume.
    (5) The air pressure in the thin glass tubes is falling.

13. Some machines obtain energy to move their parts by burning a fuel. In order for fuel to burn, it must use oxygen from the air. Which of the following machines needs air to burn fuel in order to move its parts?

    (1) power lawn mowers
    (2) coffee makers
    (3) sewing machines
    (4) televisions
    (5) vacuum cleaners

14. When fuels are burned, the energy used causes the resulting gases to expand and push on mechanical moving parts. In which of the following vehicles is the entire vehicle moved by the expanding gases rather than moving parts within the vehicle?

    (1) rocket ships
    (2) diesel engines with pistons
    (3) airplane turbines
    (4) steam engines on trains
    (5) a motorbike with a gasoline engine

15. A lever is a type of simple machine. It transmits a force at one point along its length when a force is applied at another point, while the whole lever pivots at a third point. Which of the following devices makes use of a lever?

    (1) nut and bolt
    (2) wheelbarrow
    (3) ramp
    (4) hammer
    (5) pulley

16. When the source of a sound is in motion relative to the person who hears the sound, the person will notice an apparent change in the sound's pitch. This is called the Doppler effect. The apparent change in pitch is caused by the compression of the sound waves as the source of the sound nears (the pitch gets higher), and their elongation as the source moves away (the pitch gets lower).

In which of the following circumstances would the pitch sound higher?

    (1) a piano is played in the next room
    (2) a police car approaches with its siren on
    (3) a person walks and talks on a cell phone
    (4) a fire engine drives away with its siren on
    (5) a smoke alarm goes off next door

Questions 17 through 19 refer to the following paragraph.

The plasma state is considered the fourth state of matter. Materials existing as solids, liquids, and gases can enter the plasma state if ionized by very high temperatures in the tens of thousands of degrees Celsius. Much matter on the sun exists in the plasma state.

17. According to the above passage, under which of the following conditions does matter enter the plasma state?

   (1) when it is in the sun
   (2) when it is preceded by a gaseous state
   (3) when its pressure is decreased
   (4) when it is heated to extreme temperatures
   (5) when it is bombarded by radiation

18. In which of the following places would one expect to find matter in the plasma state?

   (1) in microwave ovens
   (2) in conventional ovens
   (3) at the equator
   (4) on the moon
   (5) in glowing stars

19. When matter exists in a solid form, it has its own size and shape. Which of the following substances is a solid?

   (1) air in a balloon
   (2) an ice cube
   (3) molten lava
   (4) steam
   (5) a sugar solution

Question 20 refers to the following diagram.

Steam Turbine Operating a Ship's Propeller

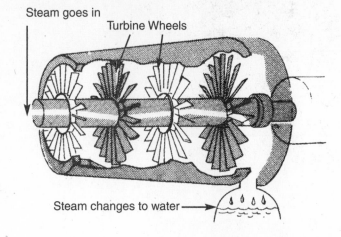

20. Gases have higher energy levels than liquids. What is the most likely reason water enters the turbine as steam but leaves as liquid water?

   (1) The energy stored in the steam was transferred to the movable turbine wheels creating motion, and the decrease in energy changed the steam to water.
   (2) The turbine wheels were cold, therefore cooling the steam.
   (3) The high pressures inside a turbine increased the speed of the water molecules and created motion.
   (4) The moving blades cut up the steam molecules into water droplets.
   (5) The moving blades acted as fans, cooling the steam.

Questions 21 through 23 refer to the following information.

As the number of known elements increased, it became cumbersome to write out their names when expressing chemical reactions. In the early 1800's, a Swedish chemist, Joens Jakob Berzelius, designed the current standardized system of scientific notation.

The capitalized first letter of the element's Latin name represents the element. If more than one element began with the same letter, a second small letter was attached.

C = carbon
Ca = calcium
Cl = chlorine
Cu = copper, Latin name cuprum

The letter symbol stands for one atom. To express two or more atoms, a numerical subscript is placed at the bottom right of that element's letter(s). The notation CO_2 means one atom of carbon with two atoms of oxygen.

21. The following word prefixes refer to numbers: mon = 1, di = 2, tri = 3, tetra = 4, and pent = 5. How would carbontetrachloride be written in scientific notation?

    (1) CCl_1
    (2) CCl_2
    (3) CCl_4
    (4) $CoCl_4$
    (5) $CuCl_4$

22. The notation CO_2 would be identified as which of the following?

    (1) carbon dioxide
    (2) carbon monoxide
    (3) carbon pentoxide
    (4) carbon tetroxide
    (5) carbon trioxide

23. If H = hydrogen, O = oxygen, C = carbon, and if hydrocarbon fuels contain only hydrogen and carbon, which of the following formulas is a hydrocarbon?

    (1) CH_4
    (2) $C_6H_{12}O_6$
    (3) H_2CO_3
    (4) $C_6H_{13}OH$
    (5) H_2COOH

Questions 24 and 25 refer to the following diagram.

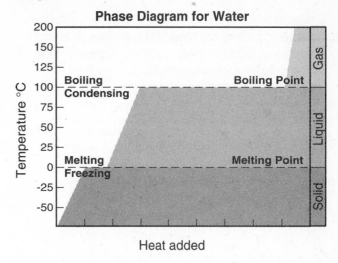

24. How does the melting temperature of solid water compare to the freezing temperature of liquid water?

    (1) The melting temperature is 100° higher than the freezing temperature.
    (2) The melting temperature is slightly higher than the freezing temperature.
    (3) The melting and freezing temperatures are the same.
    (4) The melting temperature is slightly lower than the freezing temperature.
    (5) The two temperatures cannot be compared.

25. According to the diagram, what happens when heat is applied to water to make it boil?

    The temperature of the water

    (1) stays the same throughout the time the water is boiling
    (2) rises slightly during the time the water is boiling
    (3) decreases during the time the water is boiling
    (4) rises sharply during time the water is boiling
    (5) rises sharply after the water starts boiling and then levels off

Questions 26 through 29 refer to the following information.

A mixture is a combination of substances held together by physical means. Many raw materials are mixtures. Industries separate ingredients by taking advantage of differences in physical properties. The following methods are only some of the ways mixtures can be separated.

extraction—placing a mixture in water or another solvent to dissolve one of its components, filtering off the liquid and then evaporating the solvent, leaving the previously dissolved substance

distillation—vaporizing the mixture and collecting the ingredients as they reliquefy at different temperatures

sorting—selecting the desired ingredients from a fragmented mixture by hand or machine to capture particles according to the size or visual characteristics desired

magnetic separation—using magnets to separate mixtures; the non-magnetic waste drops off, leaving the desired ingredient

gravitation—separating a mixture by the density of the ingredients; the substance with the greatest density settles to the bottom while the substance with the least density remains at the top

26. A series of sieves with different hole sizes is used to separate soil into components of specific grain size. This describes which process of separation?

(1) extraction
(2) distillation
(3) sorting
(4) magnetic separation
(5) gravitation

27. Petroleum is heated to a vapor. As the vapor cools, kerosene, gasoline, and other products are collected at their different condensation points. This describes which process of separation?

(1) extraction
(2) distillation
(3) sorting
(4) magnetic separation
(5) gravitation

28. Iron ore is separated from waste rock by exposing the mixture to a wide electromagnetic belt. The waste falls away, while the iron ore clings to the belt. This describes which process of separation?

(1) extraction
(2) distillation
(3) sorting
(4) magnetic separation
(5) gravitation

29. A solid substance dissolved in a liquid can be separated out simply by evaporating the liquid. This method is used to obtain which of the following?

(1) salt from sea water
(2) oxygen from air
(3) carbon dioxide from water
(4) alcohol from water
(5) lubricating oil from petroleum

30. Absolute zero is the theoretical temperature at which all molecular motion stops. It is approximately −459.67°F (or −273.16°C). This temperature has never been measured in a laboratory because the act of measurement changes the temperature of the system. However, scientists have achieved temperatures within about a millionth of a degree of absolute zero.

Based on the information above, why is absolute zero a theoretical temperature?

(1) Not all scientists agree on what the correct temperature is.
(2) It is not a valid hypothesis.
(3) Scientists need new ways of measuring temperature.
(4) Thermometers are often inaccurate.
(5) There is no experimental verification of absolute zero.

Questions 31 through 34 refer to the following information.

The lowest temperature at which a substance begins to burn and continues to burn is called its kindling temperature. A flame may provide the heat needed to start a substance burning but is not a necessary factor.

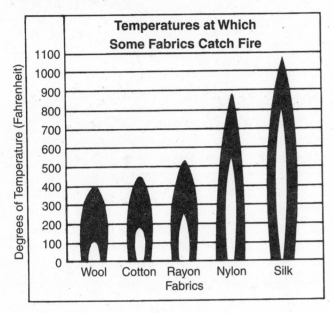

Temperatures at Which Some Fabrics Catch Fire

31. A garment made of which of the following fabrics would have the lowest kindling temperature?

    (1) cotton
    (2) nylon
    (3) rayon
    (4) silk
    (5) wool

32. Which fabric has a kindling temperature about half that of silk?

    (1) wool
    (2) cotton
    (3) rayon
    (4) nylon
    (5) silk

33. Which of the following would be the best clothing for a cook?

    (1) a short-sleeved silk shirt
    (2) a long-sleeved nylon shirt
    (3) a cotton shirt with long, flowing sleeves
    (4) a long-sleeved cotton shirt
    (5) a loose, flowing wool shirt

34. Why can wool blankets be used to cover and put out small fires?

    Because

    (1) wool has a low kindling temperature
    (2) wool has a high kindling temperature
    (3) wool absorbs water easily
    (4) the blanket prevents the burning item from reacting with the oxygen in the air
    (5) the wool blanket is rough and rubs against the burning item producing sparks

---

Question 35 refers to the following information and diagram.

A famous experiment in 1911 showed something very important about the structure of the atom. Until then, it was believed that atoms were solid spheres. The experiment (see diagram) directed alpha particles at a very thin sheet of gold foil. Surrounding the foil was a screen coated with zinc sulfide, which produced flashes of light when struck by alpha particles. Most of the alpha particles passed straight through the gold foil as if it wasn't even there. Only a few were deflected out of line.

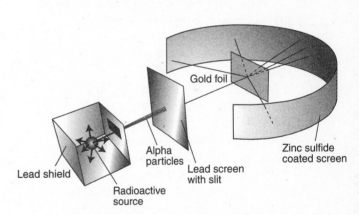

35. What did the experiment indicate about the structure of the atom?

    (1) Gold does not contain any atoms.
    (2) The alpha particles were too large.
    (3) The alpha particles were too small.
    (4) The gold foil was too thin.
    (5) Atoms are mostly empty space.

Questions 36 through 38 refer to the following passage.

Hydrogen is the lightest of all the gases. Air contains a mixture of different kinds of gases. The heaviest ones sink and are concentrated near Earth's surface. The lightest ones float to the top of the atmosphere and escape into space.

Much hydrogen gas was released into the atmosphere during the early stages of Earth's development. At present, the atmosphere contains 0.001% hydrogen.

36. Which of the following does the passage above imply about the hydrogen originally in Earth's atmosphere?

    That it

    (1) escaped into space
    (2) reacted with oxygen to form water
    (3) was present in very small amounts
    (4) is still part of the atmosphere today
    (5) was captured by the gravitational pull of the moon

37. Which statement best explains why there is so little hydrogen in the atmosphere?

    (1) Hydrogen gas unites with oxygen to form water.
    (2) Hydrogen atoms float in the air and escape into outer space.
    (3) Many hydrogen atoms are used in the formation of hydrocarbon fuels.
    (4) Carbohydrates and fats contain carbon, hydrogen, and oxygen.
    (5) The sun and other glowing stars are made primarily of hydrogen.

38. Seventy-eight percent of the air at Earth's surface is composed of nitrogen. Therefore, in the mixture called air, nitrogen is which of the following?

    It is

    (1) one of the atmosphere's heavier elements
    (2) very reactive with oxygen
    (3) not reactive with other gases
    (4) not found in the soil
    (5) essential for life

39. Moving air can act as a force and do work by pushing or pulling calm air to other areas or moving other substances. Which of the following machines does not use moving air to perform its function?

    (1) vacuum sweepers for cleaning
    (2) spray pumps for painting
    (3) sails for sailing boats
    (4) fans for cooling homes
    (5) buzz saws for cutting timber

Question 40 refers to the following paragraph.

Photovoltaic cells convert the energy of sunlight into electrical energy. They are fairly expensive to manufacture, and each cell produces a relatively tiny amount of electricity. For these reasons they are not the most cost-efficient way to provide electrical power for large numbers of people. However, using photovoltaic cells produces no harmful by-products and does not deplete our non-renewable petroleum reserves.

40. The information in the paragraph supports which conclusion?

    (1) Photovoltaic cells will never be an important source of electrical power.
    (2) Photovoltaic cells are the best way to produce electricity.
    (3) Photovoltaic cells have some advantages over fossil-fuel-burning power plants.
    (4) Photovoltaic cells are the answer to satisfying our future electric power needs.
    (5) Using photovoltaic cells to produce all our electricity will eliminate pollution.

41. Why does heating increase the rate at which water evaporates?

Because heating

(1) makes the water molecules more likely to split apart into atoms
(2) decreases the density of the water
(3) makes the water molecules more likely to form bonds with each other
(4) strips electrons from the water molecules
(5) makes water molecules at the surface more likely to break away from the rest

---

Questions 42 and 43 refer to the following information.

The destructive effects of an atomic bomb are of five types:

flash—	bright light that may temporarily or permanently blind one who watches
blast—	a shock wave that breaks objects into pieces
thermal radiation—	a release of heat over 3,000°C that vaporizes most substances
nuclear radiation—	gamma rays and neutrons that destroy living tissue
residual radioactivity—	small radioactive particles that rise high into the stratosphere, mix with the air, and fall back to Earth's surface. When humans are exposed to it, illness, death, cancer, sterility, and genetic code changes can result.

42. Which of the following effects would a group of individuals who survive a nuclear attack attempt to avoid?

(1) blast
(2) flash
(3) nuclear radiation
(4) residual radioactivity
(5) thermal radiation

43. The main effect of a nuclear attack that could cause blindness is which of the following?

(1) blast
(2) flash
(3) nuclear radiation
(4) residual radioactivity
(5) thermal radiation

Question 44 refers to the following passage.

For decades scientists have been attempting to devise a theory that would unify all the forces in the universe (gravity, strong nuclear, weak interaction, and electromagnetic) into one grand unified theory (GUT). The most promising theories are "superstring theories." Recent versions of superstring theories suggest that at the creation of the universe at least 10 (and possibly as many as 25) dimensions existed. Supporters of superstring theories say that these dimensions collapsed soon after the universe was born.

No superstring theory has yet been confirmed by experiment. Some of these theories predict that the proton, previously thought to be stable, will eventually decay. Although experiments have been conducted to detect the proton decay, it has not been seen. Since none of the superstring theories has been confirmed by experiments, it is not likely that superstring theories are at all scientifically valid.

44. Which of the following would likely convince the author of the passage that superstring theories are valid?

(1) experiments that show the effects of additional dimensions in a far-off galaxy
(2) experiments that show gravity does not exist in empty space
(3) new mathematical methods for calculating dimensions
(4) experiments that detect proton decay
(5) experiments that show the proton to be stable

Question 45 refers to the following information and illustration.

The illustration shows a person throwing a ball outward off a cliff. If gravity did not act on the ball, it would follow the straight, dotted line. But gravity does act on the ball and causes it to fall a vertical distance of 4.9 meters per second every time the ball is thrown. In fact, it is the same ball, with the same size and weight, that is thrown each time.

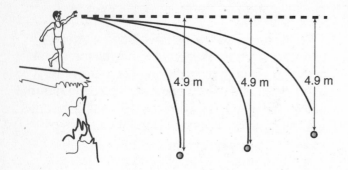

45. Based on this information, what causes the ball to travel different distances in each case as illustrated above?

(1) the steepness of the cliff
(2) the force with which the ball is thrown
(3) the variations in the force of gravity at different elevations
(4) the curvature of the earth
(5) the centrifugal force

Question 46 refers to the following information.

The pH scale shows the strength of acids and bases relative to water, which has a pH of 7. Acids and bases are defined according to their chemical properties. An acid is a substance that has a pH lower than 7. Lemon juice is a common acid; it contains citric acid. A base is a substance that has a pH higher than 7. Baking soda is a commonly-used base.

When mixed together, acids and bases can neutralize each other. When combined in the correct proportions, they form water and a salt: a neutral substance that is neither acidic nor basic.

The pH Scale

Basic

14 Lye
13
    Bleach
12 Ammonia
11
10
    Baking soda
9 Milk of magnesia
8
7 Neutral: pure water
    Milk
6
5 Black coffee
4 Tomato juice
3 Vinegar
2
    Stomach acid
1
0 Hydrochloric acid

Acidic

46. Which of the following substances would you mix with vinegar (acetic acid) to neutralize it?

(1) coffee
(2) ammonia
(3) orange juice
(4) milk
(5) rain water

Sound is caused by vibrations. If vibrations follow each other slowly, the sound has a low frequency; if they follow each other quickly, the sound has a high frequency. A sound's pitch is related to its frequency: high-pitched sounds have high frequencies and low-pitched sounds have low frequencies. Frequency is usually expressed in measurements called hertz, or Hz.

Frequency (Hz) of Musical Notes

Note	Freq (Hz)
do	264
re	297
mi	330
fa	352
sol	396
la	440
ti	495
do	528

47. You are in a choral group and are practicing singing scales with a friend. You sing "la," but your friend asks you to sing a note whose pitch is higher than "la." Which note do you sing?

    (1) re
    (2) mi
    (3) fa
    (4) sol
    (5) ti

A sonic boom results when the source of a sound is traveling faster than the speed at which the sound wave can pass through a medium. For example, a jet flying through the air produces a sonic boom when its flying speed exceeds 343 meters per second. Theoretically, a sonic boom can be produced in any medium that carries sound waves.

Speed of Sound in Various Media

Medium	Speed*
Carbon dioxide	267 mps
Air	343 mps
Hydrogen	1,315 mps
Water	1,469 mps
Iron	5,121 mps

* meters per second, mps

48. Based on the above table, to produce a sonic boom in water, what must be the minimum speed of the sound source?

    (1)   270 meters per second
    (2)   344 meters per second
    (3) 1,300 meters per second
    (4) 1,320 meters per second
    (5) 1,470 meters per second

49. When matter is heated, it expands. When matter is cooled, it contracts. Which of the following is a useful, everyday example of this phenomenon?

    (1) food kept fresh in the refrigerator
    (2) the circulation of the blood in the body
    (3) a heater blowing warm air into a room
    (4) movement of mercury in a thermometer
    (5) piston action in a car engine

Graph A
Thermal Expansion of Three Different Gases

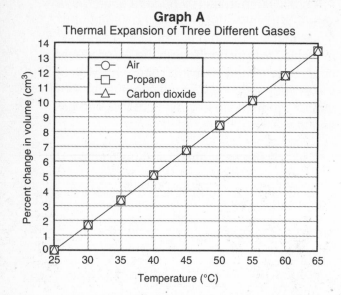

Graph B
Thermal Expansion of Three Different Liquids

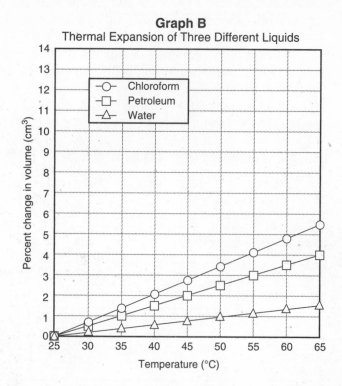

50. Charles's Law states that if the pressure remains constant, equal volumes of different gases will expand the same amount when heated. According to graph A, if a 100 cm^3 sample of gas is heated from 25°C to 55°C, how much will it expand?

It will expand by

(1) 3 cm^3
(2) 4 cm^3
(3) 5 cm^3
(4) 10 cm^3
(5) 50 cm^3

51. Which of the following statements best summarizes the differences between Graph A and Graph B?

(1) Expansion by heat is dependent on the kind of liquid but independent of the kind of gas.
(2) Liquids expand more when heated than gases at the same temperature.
(3) The gases tested were mixed together but the liquids were tested individually.
(4) For an equal temperature increase, air and water have the same percent volume increase.
(5) The volume of a gas is dependent on temperature, but the volume of a liquid is independent of temperature.

52. The laws of nature are universal. If a space probe to the planet Venus returns a sample of the gases in Venus's atmosphere to Earth, which of the following results would be expected upon heating the sample?

(1) The gases would explode violently.
(2) The gases would contract.
(3) The gases would not change as Venus is hotter than Earth.
(4) The gases would expand in conformance to Charles's Law.
(5) The gases in the sample will expand at a different rate if they are separated.

53. A 100 cm^3 sample of an unknown liquid at 25°C is heated to 55°C. What will most likely happen to the volume of the liquid?

It will

(1) be unchanged
(2) increase by 3 cm^3
(3) increase by 10 cm^3
(4) increase by an unknown amount
(5) decrease by an unknown amount

Question 54 refers to the following information and diagram.

During the spin cycle in a washing machine, the inside tub rotates very quickly. The spinning tub exerts an inward-directed force on the clothes. This force keeps them oriented toward the center of the tub.

There are also holes in the tub—holes large enough to permit water to escape. The water is free to flow out of the holes, so your clothes do not come out sopping wet.

54. Which of the following operates on clothes during a washing machine spin cycle?

   (1) the force of gravity, which pulls objects toward Earth
   (2) the centripetal force, which pulls rotating objects inward toward a center
   (3) angular momentum, in which an object will maintain its angle of motion unless acted upon by an unbalanced force
   (4) the centrifugal force, which pulls rotating objects away from the center
   5) inertia, which is an object's resistance to changing its motion

55. A certain chemical compound is used as a food additive. Which of the following statements best supports a claim that this compound is harmless to people?

   (1) The elements in the compound are all known to be harmless by themselves.
   (2) The compound occurs in nature.
   (3) Another compound made up of the same elements is known to be harmless.
   (4) No one has become ill after eating a food containing the compound.
   (5) Rats fed large amounts of the compound showed no ill effects over several generations.

Question 56 refers to the following passage.

Every time you open a refrigerator door, you use electricity. In fact, standing in front of an open refrigerator wastes an enormous amount of electricity. It is estimated that in many American homes, the refrigerator door is held ajar for about 1 hour each day. The average size refrigerator uses 7 kilowatts per hour of electricity, at a cost of about 14 cents per kilowatt hour.

56. Approximately how much does 1 hour per day of standing in front of an open refrigerator cost a family in one year?

   (1) $255
   (2) $ 51
   (3) $ 98
   (4) $357
   (5) $766

Question 57 refers to the following passage.

When molecules of a gas are compressed, or forced closer together, they move around more rapidly and collide with each other frequently. Heat is a measure of the average motion of molecules. In this way, compression creates heat.

57. Which of the following actions is an example of this phenomenon?

   (1) an air pump getting hotter as it inflates a football
   (2) a car's gas tank overflowing when it is topped off
   (3) an electric heater warming the air in a closed room
   (4) gases or liquids under pressure in an aerosol can
   (5) a car tire heating up when the car is driven in the summer

Questions 58 through 61 refer to the following information.

Following are some examples of how Newton's laws of motion affect our daily lives.

   A. It takes more gasoline to speed up a heavily loaded truck from 40 m.p.h. to 50 m.p.h. than it does to accelerate a small car the same amount.
   B. All cars are equipped with brakes to apply the force necessary to stop.
   C. Water squirting from a lawn sprinkler pushes the metal spinner backward, causing it to rotate.
   D. When someone steps ashore from a rowboat, the boat slips backward.
   E. A bicycle has gears to make going uphill easier.

58. Newton's First Law of Motion states that a body in motion will stay in motion unless a force acts upon it. Which of the examples given above illustrates this law?

   (1) A
   (2) B
   (3) C
   (4) D
   (5) E

59. Newton's Second Law of Motion states that the larger the mass, the greater its resistance to a change in velocity. Which of the examples given above illustrates this law?

   (1) A
   (2) B
   (3) C
   (4) D
   (5) E

60. Newton's Third Law of Motion states that for every action, there is an equal and opposite reaction. Which of the examples given above illustrates this law?

   (1) A and B
   (2) B and E
   (3) C and D
   (4) A and E
   (5) E only

61. Which of the following examples illustrates the same law of motion as Example B?

   (1) Water evaporates in the sun.
   (2) Earth continues to revolve around the sun.
   (3) A gun recoils when fired.
   (4) Water flows faster when it enters a narrower pipe.
   (5) A heavy object is moved more easily with a lever.

Questions 62 through 64 refer to the following paragraph.

To produce sound, matter vibrates. In string instruments, the strings vibrate. Percussion instruments are struck to vibrate. Brass instruments have metal valves or a slide to change vibrating air columns. Wind instruments have holes that, when covered, change vibrating air columns. Wind instruments may also have a vibrating reed.

62. To which group of instruments would the bass tuba and trumpet belong?

   (1) brass
   (2) percussion
   (3) strings
   (4) vibrator
   (5) wind

63. To which group of instruments do guitars and banjos belong?

   (1) brass
   (2) folk
   (3) percussion
   (4) strings
   (5) wind

64. What produces sound by vibrating when a gong is struck by a mallet?

   (1) the hands of the player
   (2) the mallet
   (3) the gong
   (4) the frame holding the gong
   (5) the strings suspending the gong

Questions 65 through 67 refer to the following passage.

Constants do not change whereas variables do change. Independent variables change on their own while dependent variables change only in response to changes of another variable. Amedeo Avogadro came to the conclusion that for equal volumes, all gases contained the same number of molecules if the temperature and pressure on the gas were the same. Avogadro estimated this number to be 602,000,000,000,000,000,000,000 (or 6.02×10^{23}). This number came to be called Avogadro's number and is used in many calculations involving gases.

65. Avogadro's number is a constant. Therefore, which of the following is true?

Avogadro's number

(1) will increase in proportion to the amount measured
(2) will decrease as the volume increases
(3) will depend on the dependent variable
(4) will depend on the independent variable
(5) will not change

66. A decrease in the amount of acid added to a specific volume of water will lessen the concentration of the solution. Which statement indicates the relationship of the amount of acid to the concentration of the solution?

(1) The concentration is a constant.
(2) The concentration depends on the amount of acid.
(3) The amount of solution depends on the concentration of the acid.
(4) The solution is concentrated when the acid is concentrated.
(5) There is no relationship between the amount of acid and the concentration.

67. The greater the surface area exposed to air, the faster water from a boiling solution can evaporate into the air. After a liquid has boiled for a time, what happens to the amount of water left in the container?

It

(1) is the independent variable
(2) is a constant
(3) is dependent on the type of solution
(4) is dependent on the surface area exposed
(5) is independent of the amount of water originally in the container

Question 68 refers to the following information and illustration.

A material's density is its mass per unit of volume—or how much matter is packed into a given volume of space. As the illustration shows, materials with a lower density will float on top of other materials with a higher density. The density per cubic centimeter (cm^3) is given for every material in the container except one—the layer of plastic.

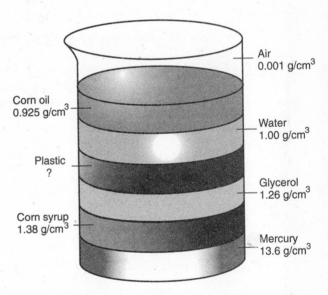

68. Which of the following densities does the plastic have?

(1) 0.06 g/cm^3
(2) 0.98 g/cm^3
(3) 1.17 g/cm^3
(4) 1.32 g/cm^3
(5) 1.41 g/cm^3

Questions 69 and 70 refer to the following information.

Cars and trucks have induction coils to boost the voltage of the electricity from the battery to the spark plugs. Batteries produce direct current of rather low voltage. To increase the voltage, a primary coil and a secondary coil are wound around an iron core. The secondary coil will have a much larger voltage because of the greater number of turns in the wire.

Electricity produced at power plants is alternating current. To push the current through long distances, the voltage must be high. This high voltage is too dangerous to use in households so when it nears the customer, the voltage is decreased to 120 volts. A device to step up or step down the voltage of alternating current is called a transformer. Transformers are designed like induction coils with an iron core surrounding primary and secondary coils.

69. A van or bus would have which of the following devices to supply high voltage current?

(1) stabilizer
(2) induction coil
(3) battery
(4) step-up transformer
(5) step-down transformer

70. In many foreign countries, the electrical power supplied is 240 volts. When American tourists take electric razors or hairdryers to Europe, they must place which of the following devices between the appliance and the electrical outlet?

(1) battery
(2) dry cell
(3) induction coil
(4) step-up transformer
(5) step-down transformer

An Induction Coil

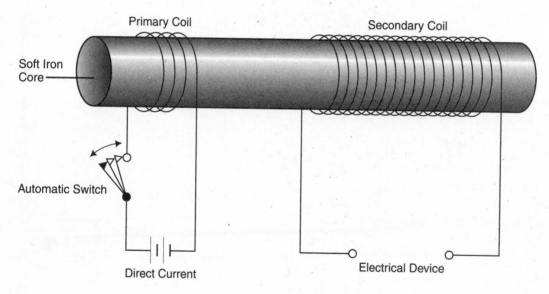

Static electricity is a charge on an object that has collected extra electrons by rubbing against a second object. Static electricity is not very useful. When a charge that has built up on an object comes near or touches an object with insufficient electrons, the object discharges the extra electrons. More electrons must then be collected, usually by rubbing them off another object, before there can be another instance of transfer.

Electric current is the continual flow of electrons. The flow is transferred by metal wires. Gold, platinum, and silver are excellent metals for wires; however, their cost prohibits their use for the distribution of electricity to households throughout the United States. They are, however, used in extremely sensitive circuits such as computers and in instances where repair is difficult or costly. Lead and aluminum wiring were found to overheat, melt, and cause fires if large amounts of current were used by a household. Iron lacked the flexibility necessary to withstand the bending motion of electrical cords.

Copper was found to be the cost-effective choice for general electrical usage and is used extensively throughout the world. It too can overheat, melt, and cause fires but not as quickly as aluminum. As a safety precaution, fuses are required in all circuit installations. Fuses prevent fires by stopping current flow before melting can occur in the wire.

71. Why does consumer usage depend on current rather than static electricity?

Because

(1) the charge of static electricity is too great
(2) the rubbing needed to produce static electricity is not cost-effective
(3) the flow of electrons is not continuous with static electricity
(4) the continuous flow of current electricity is too dangerous
(5) the static discharge cannot use fuses to prevent fires

72. Which of the following metals would most likely be used in the wiring of space shuttles and satellites?

(1) gold and silver
(2) lead and aluminum
(3) copper and iron
(4) lead and copper
(5) aluminum and copper

73. Who would benefit most from the improper installation and use of fuses?

(1) the original building contractors who want to meet city regulations
(2) the homeowners who do not wish to risk the lives of family members
(3) the county budget office that must pay for the maintenance of a fire department
(4) the contractors who repair the damage or demolish the structure and rebuild a new home
(5) the insurance company that insures a home

Question 74 refers to the following information.

Atoms of different elements bond together to form molecules. The diagrams below show the bond structure in several kinds of organic molecule groups (hydroxyl, aldehyde, carbonyl, ether, and carboxyl). A double bond is represented by a double line between elements.

Name of Group	Structure
Hydroxyl	— OH
Aldehyde	$-C\underset{H}{\overset{\nearrow O}{}}$
Carbonyl	$-\overset{O}{\underset{}{C}}-$
Ether	$-C-O-C-$
Carboxyl	$-C\overset{OH}{\underset{O}{}}$

74. Which organic molecule structure(s) show a double bond?

(1) aldehyde only
(2) aldehyde and hydroxyl
(3) carbonyl, hydroxyl, ether
(4) aldehyde and ether
(5) aldehyde, carbonyl, and carboxyl

SCIENCE

Directions

The Science Simulated Test consists of multiple-choice questions intended to measure your understanding of general concepts in science. The questions are based on short readings or on graphs, charts, or diagrams. Study the information given, and then answer the questions that follow. Refer to the information as often as necessary in answering the questions.

You should spend no more than 80 minutes answering the 50 questions on the Science Simulated Test. Work carefully, but do not spend too much time on any one question. Do not skip any items. Make a reasonable guess when you are not sure of an answer. You will not be penalized for incorrect answers.

When time is up, mark the last item you finished. This will tell you whether you can finish the real GED Test in the time allowed. Then complete the test.

Record your answers to the questions on a copy of the answer sheet on page 110. Be sure that all required information is properly recorded on the answer sheet.

To record your answers, mark the numbered space on the answer sheet that corresponds to the answer you choose for each question on the test.

Example:

Which of the following is the smallest unit in a living thing?

(1) tissue
(2) organ
(3) cell
(4) muscle
(5) capillary

The correct answer is "cell;" therefore, answer space 3 should be marked on the answer sheet.

Do not rest the point of your pencil on the answer sheet while you are considering your answer. Make no stray or unnecessary marks. If you change an answer, erase your first mark completely. Mark only one answer space for each question; multiple answers will be scored as incorrect. Do not fold or crease your answer sheet.

When you finish the test, use the Analysis of Performance Chart on page 69 to determine whether you are ready to take the real GED Test, and, if not, which skill areas need additional review.

Adapted with permission of the American Council on Education.

Directions: Choose the one best answer to each question.

Question 1 refers to the following graph.

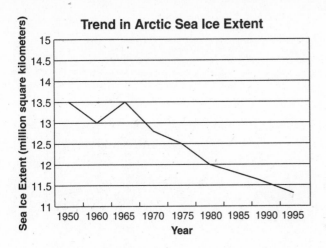

Trend in Arctic Sea Ice Extent

1. Most scientists believe that global warming is causing major changes in many parts of the world, including the melting of sea ice in the Arctic. About how many million square kilometers of sea ice were lost in the Arctic between 1950 and 1995?

   (1) 12
   (2) 2.3
   (3) 11.1
   (4) 3.5
   (5) 0.5

Question 2 refers to the following information.

   Mirrors reflect light in real or distorted ways depending on the curvature of their surface. Prisms break light into the visible spectrum, revealing a rainbow of colors. Lenses bend light and can be made to focus light and/or seem to increase or decrease an object's size.

2. Which of the following glass objects would be part of a pair of eyeglasses to increase visual observation at normal distances?

   (1) flat mirrors
   (2) curved mirrors
   (3) triangular prisms
   (4) right angle prisms
   (5) lenses

3. Fisheries experts routinely place size limits on fish that can be harvested. There is an important reason for this. If undersized fish are harvested, there will not be a sufficient number of reproducing adults to sustain the fish population.

   Which of the following is implied by this information?

   (1) Harvesting small fish is unprofitable.
   (2) All harvested fish grow to a large size.
   (3) Small adult fish cannot reproduce.
   (4) Fish must be 6 inches long before they can be harvested.
   (5) Fish size is correlated with maturity and reproductive age.

Question 4 refers to the following information.

Flowering plants are classified by their life cycle and their hardiness. These categories are:

Annual	completes life cycle—germination, growth, flowering, and death—in one growing season
Biennial	completes life cycle in two growing seasons
Perennial	life cycle lasts for a number of years, with plant flowering each year
Tender	sensitive to the cold
Hardy	able to withstand frost

4. The coleus plant can live outdoors from early spring through late fall, even in northern climates. Its seed must be planted anew each spring. Which categories describe the coleus?

   (1) annual and tender
   (2) biennial and tender
   (3) perennial and hardy
   (4) perennial and tender
   (5) annual and hardy

Food Chain

Snake eaten
by hawk

Frog eaten
by snake

Grasshopper
eaten by frog

5. What is the most noticeable characteristic of the order of the animals in this food chain?

   (1) means of locomotion
   (2) length
   (3) size
   (4) speed
   (5) eye type

6. What is the major advantage of being at the top of a food chain?

   (1) All those below are easier to catch.
   (2) The top animal can be seen more easily.
   (3) The top animal has fewer predators.
   (4) The top animal can fly.
   (5) The bottom animal can hide more easily.

Question 7 refers to the following graph.

Causes of World Desertification

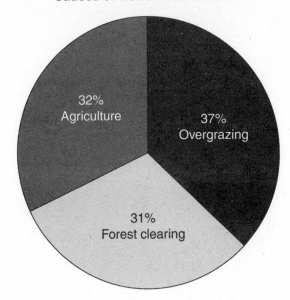

- 32% Agriculture
- 37% Overgrazing
- 31% Forest clearing

7. Desertification is the process in which land is degraded and soil is lost to erosion. Based on the chart, which of the following policies would have the greatest positive impact on the problem of desertification?

(1) restricting significantly the number of animals grazing on range land
(2) requiring most farms to use organic farming methods
(3) banning the clearing of forests
(4) having farmers plant more legumes, which add nutrients to soil
(5) promoting grazing on agricultural land

8. This chemical formula shows the process by which sulfur oxides combine with water to form acid rain.

$$SO_3 + H_2O \longrightarrow H_2SO_4$$

What is the ratio between the number of sulfur oxide molecules and the number of water molecules in the formula?

(1) 1 to 1
(2) 3 to 2
(3) 3 to 1
(4) 1 to 2
(5) 5 to 6

Question 9 refers to the following passage.

In January 2000, scientists released satellite photos of the surface of Mars. The photos showed land forms that appeared to be formed of sedimentary rock—rock that is formed from accumulated layers of silt and sediment that have compacted and hardened under their own weight. Some newspapers reported this as proof that Mars has, or had, water, because on Earth, sedimentary rock is often formed from sediments in lakes or rivers. The papers also suggested that fossils occur in the Martian rock.

9. Which of the following is an unstated assumption in the conclusion that Mars has water?

(1) Gravity has the same affect on Mars as on Earth.
(2) There was no lake in the picture of Mars.
(3) Sedimentary rock on Mars forms in the same way that sedimentary rock forms on Earth.
(4) Fossils occur in igneous rock.
(5) No fossil fish were found on Mars.

Questions 10 through 12 refer to the following illustration.

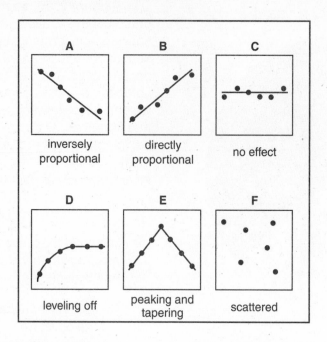

10. A company wishes to show that its nuclear power reactors have not in any way endangered the lives of people in areas surrounding the nuclear power plants. Which graph would best reflect this contention?

(1) A
(2) B
(3) C
(4) D
(5) E

11. Which of the graph types would be used by an environmental lobbyist attempting to show the amount of animal life remaining as an oil spill invades a bay?

(1) A
(2) B
(3) C
(4) E
(5) F

12. After being heated, a cold solution at 0°C reached its boiling point at 87.5°C. Further heating did not increase the liquid's temperature beyond that point. Which graph would best illustrate the heating of the liquid?

(1) A
(2) B
(3) C
(4) D
(5) E

Question 13 refers to the following table.

World Population Growth

Year	World Population (in billions)	Number of Years Since Last Billion Added
0	0.30	
1804	1.00	
1927	2.00	123 years
1930	2.07	
1940	2.30	
1950	2.52	
1960	3.02	33 years
1970	3.70	
1974	4.00	14 years
1980	4.44	
1987	5.00	13 years
1990	5.27	
1999	6.00	12 years

13. Based on the table, approximately how many years will it take to add one billion people to the 1999 world population?

    (1)   1 year
    (2) 11 years
    (3) 25 years
    (4) 39 years
    (5) 120 years

Question 14 refers to the following passage.

In 1596, a Dutch mapmaker drew a map of Earth in which he showed how North and South America could fit neatly around Europe and Africa, forming one large landmass. In 1858, a geographer found and redrew this map. He published the map to illustrate his theory that, at one time, the Americas, Europe, Asia, and Africa had been joined in a single, giant landmass, but had later been torn apart by powerful forces within the earth. In 1912, a German meteorologist who had studied the 1858 map used it to support his revolutionary theory of "continental drift." This theory stated that 200 million years ago, the earth's huge supercontinent split apart. This theory was proven true when scientists later discovered that the earth's crust is divided into plates that move over the earth, carrying landmasses with them.

14. Which of the following statements describes the important process in scientific inquiry that led to the modern theory of plate tectonics?

    (1) Accurate maps were drawn in the 1500s.
    (2) Africa and Europe are joined by tectonic plates.
    (3) Scientific knowledge is gained only through trial and error.
    (4) The theory of continental drift was later proved wrong.
    (5) Scientific knowledge is built on previous theories and discoveries.

Question 15 refers to the following graph.

Population of Adult Atlantic Salmon, 1975–1998

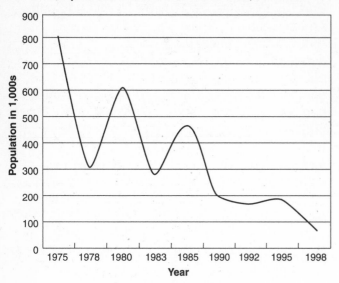

15. The Atlantic salmon is proposed as an addition to the list of endangered species. What information do you need in order to assess whether the Atlantic salmon deserves such status?

   (1) the normal population trends for Pacific salmon
   (2) the number of Atlantic salmon in a normal, healthy population
   (3) the number of juveniles in the 1998 population of Atlantic salmon
   (4) the number of juveniles in the 1975 population of Atlantic salmon
   (5) the cause of the increase in population that occurred in 1980

Question 16 refers to the following passage.

   The region of stratospheric ozone depletion over the Antarctic is expanding. The atmosphere's ozone layer prevents harmful ultraviolet (UV) rays from reaching Earth. In 2000, dangerously low levels of ozone were detected over the southern parts of Australia and South America. Humans who live in areas of depleted ozone have a greater incidence of skin cancer. Ozone depletion in the atmosphere is a serious threat to human health.

16. Which of the following statements supports the conclusion that ozone depletion is harmful to health?

   (1) Antarctic penguins are starving.
   (2) Ozone depletion is caused by pollutants put into the air by humans.
   (3) Some UV rays from the sun have always hit Earth.
   (4) Eye cataracts are caused by increased exposure to UV light.
   (5) Skin cancer has many different causes.

Question 17 refers to the following information.

Chemicals called allergens occur in many household substances. Allergens can be found in mold spores, pollen, dust, dandruff, and pet hair. Many foods, especially chocolate, eggs, cow's milk, wheat, and shellfish also contain allergens. People who are sensitive to certain allergens respond to the chemicals by producing histamine which causes capillaries to enlarge, mucous glands to secrete, and smooth muscle to tighten. The enlarged capillaries cause hives, headaches, and other tissue swelling. The nasal drip of allergic rhinitis and the phlegm produced in the bronchial tubes of asthmatics are excess gland secretions. The tightening of the smooth muscle may cause the upset of the entire gastrointestinal tract.

To diagnose a particular allergy, needles are treated with chemicals from suspect substances. The needles are used to place the substances under the skin. Records are kept of the location of each substance injected. If a red patch appears where the skin is pricked, an allergy to that substance is indicated.

There is no cure for allergies. Avoidance of the known allergen is the best treatment. For some allergy sufferers, this simply means getting rid of a pet or not eating shellfish. For others, avoidance may be almost impossible, as in allergies to ragweed pollen or house dust. In severe attack cases, doctors called allergists may prescribe antihistamine drugs or attempt to desensitize the person by introducing small but constant levels of allergens into the bloodstream.

17. Which statement best explains why a nasal drip accompanies hay fever?

(1) The nose is unusually sensitive to allergens.
(2) Children who have hay fever usually have parents who are also allergic to the allergen.
(3) The capillaries in the nose enlarge in response to histamine production by the body.
(4) Histamine produced by the body in response to allergens causes mucous glands to oversecrete.
(5) Avoidance of allergens is almost impossible for hay fever sufferers.

18. An electric motor turns electrical energy into mechanical motion. Which of the following appliances best illustrates an application of the above statement?

(1) fluorescent lighting
(2) radio and TV
(3) blenders and mixers
(4) refrigerators and freezers
(5) curling irons and toasters

Question 19 refers to the following chart.

Types of Mixtures

aerosol	a suspension of a liquid in a gas
gel	a suspension of a liquid in a solid
tincture	a substance dissolved in alcohol
amalgam	the mixture of another metal with mercury
biocolloid	particles suspended in a liquid within a living organism

19. Alloys are mixtures of two or more metals. Based on the chart, which type of mixture could form an alloy?

(1) aerosol
(2) gel
(3) tincture
(4) amalgam
(5) biocolloid

Questions 20 and 21 refer to the following graph.

Maximum Water Held by Air

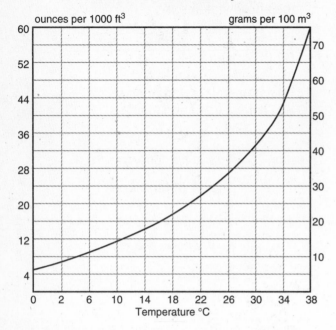

20. Approximately how much water, in grams per 100 m³, can air hold at a temperature of 10°C?

   (1) 8
   (2) 11
   (3) 14
   (4) 20
   (5) 48

21. To reduce the amount of water held by the air from 44 ounces per 1000 ft³ to 12 ounces per 1000 ft³, how many degrees Celsius must the temperature be lowered?

   (1) 20
   (2) 24
   (3) 32
   (4) 40
   (5) 56

Question 22 refers to the following passage.

   Computer models of the effects of global warming indicate that as sea surface temperatures rise, more water from the ocean's surface will evaporate and form clouds. As clouds move over cooler regions, the water vapor will condense and eventually fall as rain.

22. To determine if, in fact, this process is occurring, which of the following types of data should be collected over a period of time?

   (1) the movement of ocean currents
   (2) the degree of cloud cover over the equator
   (3) the amount of rainfall over cooler regions
   (4) the number of hurricanes forming in the eastern Atlantic
   (5) the number of floods in the tropics

Question 23 refers to the following passage.

   Carnivorous plants, such as the Venus flytrap, are adapted to catch and "eat" insects. These plants have an aroma that attracts insects such as files. When the insect lands on the plant's sticky surface, it is caught and then digested by the plant. Carnivorous plants, which occur primarily in bogs, devour insects to get nutrients otherwise unavailable to them.

23. Which of the following statements supports the conclusion that carnivorous plants must eat insects to survive?

   (1) Carnivorous plants have digestive juices similar to those in animals.
   (2) The soil in bogs has extremely few nutrients.
   (3) Without carnivorous plants, bogs would be overrun with insects.
   (4) Nearly all plants that occur in bogs are carnivorous.
   (5) Bog plants are not pollinated by insects.

Questions 24 through 27 refer to the following information.

Instruments are essential to scientific investigation because the human body has (1) no detectors for certain forms of energy, (2) limited sensors for specific sizes, distances, and vibrations, and (3) limited ability to accurately measure what is observed. Instruments are designed for specific tasks that increase the range and accuracy of observation. The following instruments are examples of many used by scientists to obtain information that is otherwise unavailable.

Instrument	Use
microscope	to make small objects appear larger
oscilloscope	to see variations of electrical current as wavy lines on a screen
periscope	to get a view from a level above that of the eyes
spectroscope	to identify elements by analyzing the arrangement and amount of colored light emitted by an element
telescope	to make distant objects appear nearer and larger

24. What type of instrument are binoculars used at a football game or opera?

    A type of

    (1) microscope
    (2) oscilloscope
    (3) periscope
    (4) spectroscope
    (5) telescope

25. What type of instrument is the screen of a heart monitor displaying the electrical activity of a patient in intensive care?

    A type of

    (1) microscope
    (2) oscilloscope
    (3) periscope
    (4) spectroscope
    (5) telescope

26. A throat culture is obtained from a patient and allowed to grow. What type of instrument would be used to view a sample of the culture in order to verify the presence of streptococci bacteria?

    (1) microscope
    (2) oscilloscope
    (3) periscope
    (4) spectroscope
    (5) telescope

27. An astronomer publishes an article in which the composition of the sun is purported to be mostly hydrogen and helium. What instrument did the astronormer probably use to reach this conclusion?

    (1) microscope
    (2) oscilloscope
    (3) periscope
    (4) spectroscope
    (5) telescope

Question 28 refers to the following information.

A doctor instructed a diabetic patient to use a glucose strip indicator twice a day in the following manner.

1. Place one drop of blood on the strip, and wait 2 minutes.

2. Wipe off the blood, and compare the top and bottom colors to those listed below.

3. Perform the action suggested by the matching colors.

Colors	Action
light tan pale blue	eat a sugar substance immediately
tan blue	normal, no action required
light green blue	restrict sugar and carbohydrate intake
dark green bright blue	call the doctor for an appointment
black dark blue	go directly to the hospital

28. A blood sample was tested and the strip indicator turned tan over blue. What would the patient do?

    (1) call the doctor and arrange for an appointment
    (2) follow normal eating patterns
    (3) eat a substance containing sugar immediately
    (4) severely limit foods containing sugar
    (5) be driven to the nearest hospital

29. Organic means must contain carbon, inorganic means non-living, astro means among the stars, bio means life, and engineering means science of machines and structures. What would the study of the chemicals in body cells, fluids, and gases most likely be called?

    (1) chemical engineering
    (2) astrochemistry
    (3) biochemistry
    (4) organic chemistry
    (5) inorganic chemistry

30. As you watch distant fireworks, you notice that you hear the sound of the explosions a few seconds after you see the flashes of light. What can you infer from this observation?

    (1) sound energy and light energy travel at the same speeds
    (2) sound energy travels faster than light energy
    (3) light energy travels faster than sound energy
    (4) light energy travels in a straight line but sound energy does not
    (5) ears process information faster than eyes

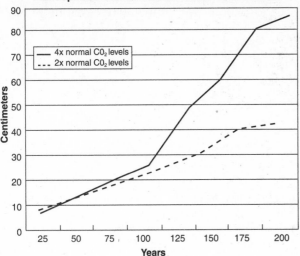

Sea Level Rise for Different Concentrations of Atmospheric Carbon Dioxide in the Next 200 Years

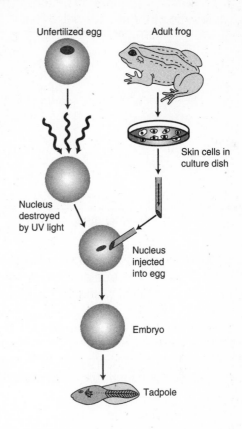

31. A 50 centimeter rise in sea level would flood the homes of 5 percent of the people on low-lying Tongatapu Island in the Pacific Ocean. If atmospheric carbon dioxide levels rise to four times that of normal, in about how many years will these Tongan homes be flooded?

    (1) 80
    (2) 100
    (3) 125
    (4) 200
    (5) 200

32. Osmosis is the process by which a liquid passes through a permeable membrane from a region with a high concentration of a substance to a region with a low concentration. Scientists are adapting the process of osmosis for practical applications. In particular, they are developing membranes that selectively trap specific substances, preventing them from passing through the membrane.

    Which of the following is an application of osmosis technology?

    (1) reducing flood damage along rivers
    (2) increasing water retention of soils
    (3) improving the circulation of the blood
    (4) filtering pollutants out of drinking water
    (5) changing the acidity of rainfall

When an animal is cloned from another animal, it is identical to its parent and shares all of its parent's genetic information. During the cloning process, the nucleus of a cell from the parent organism is inserted into an unfertilized egg that does not have a nucleus. The DNA from the parent cell's nucleus guides the development of the egg from embryo to offspring.

33. Why must the nucleus of the unfertilized egg be destroyed before the parent cell's nucleus is inserted?

    (1) because the genetic material from the egg's nucleus must be eliminated
    (2) beacuse the parent cell may contain genetic mutations
    (3) because the egg's nucleus is fertilized
    (4) because the egg's nucleus can be fertilized by the skin cell's nucleus
    (5) because the egg's nucleus is already partially developed

Question 34 refers to the following graph.

Wavelengths of Light

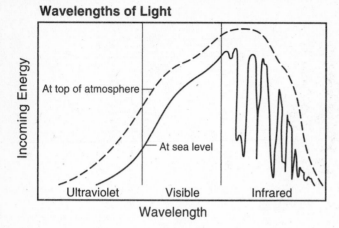

34. Compared to plants growing on Earth, plants grown in a space satellite orbiting Earth would receive which of the following?

    (1) less ultraviolet light energy
    (2) less infrared light energy
    (3) less of all light energy wavelengths
    (4) more of all light energy wavelengths
    (5) more of some infrared light wavelengths only

Question 35 refers to the following passage.

Scientists cannot study the deep interior of Earth directly, but they can use seismic waves generated by earthquakes. By noting the different speeds of seismic waves passing through each of Earth's layers, scientists have discovered that the inner core of Earth is solid and the outer core is liquid.

35. Which of the following can you conclude from the information in the passage?

    (1) The inner and outer core of Earth are very large.
    (2) A seismic wave's speed changes as it passes through different materials.
    (3) Seismic waves cannot travel through the solid inner core of Earth.
    (4) The material that makes up the liquid outer core emerges through volcanoes.
    (5) A seismic wave's speed depends on the size of the earthquake that produces it.

Question 36 refers to the following diagram and passage.

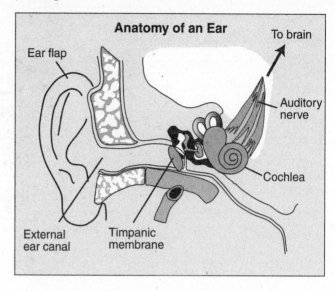

Anatomy of an Ear

Long-term exposure to very loud noises destroys the hair-like nerve endings, called cilia, which are found in the fluid-filled cochlea of the inner ear. Cilia change sound vibrations into messages that are sent to the brain. The brain interprets these signals. Scientists have found that listening to loud music, especially through headphones, destroys the cilia and leads to serious hearing distortion.

36. Based on the diagram, destroyed cilia send distorted messages to the brain via what ear organ?

    (1) the eardrum
    (2) the auditory nerve
    (3) the ear canal
    (4) the timpanic membrane
    (5) the ear flap

Natural selection is the way nature chooses which organisms survive. Chance mutations occur in response to chemicals or certain kinds of energy in the electromagnetic spectrum. If the mutant is better adapted to the environment, it thrives. If not, it dies out or becomes rare.

Humans have used artificial selection to produce plants and animals with desirable characteristics. Many of these domesticated plants and animals can no longer survive in the wild. Their survival depends on the maintenance of an artificial environment and the desires of people.

People select certain desired traits such as color, beauty, or scent (as in roses). Other traits that are bred artificially include uniqueness (as in the neck plumage of the prized Jacobin pigeon), size (as in miniature horses), meat quality or milk yield (as in cattle), or resistance to disease (as in fungus-resistant tomatoes). The traits usually are selected for convenience, pleasure, or financial gain of individuals. In this way, humans act as agents of evolution through artificial selection.

Individual specimens with the desired traits are crossbred. The hybrid offspring are then inbred to preserve and fix the desirable characteristics and eliminate unfavorable characteristics from the stock.

A pure breed is formed when there is not any mixture of other genes over many generations. The American Kennel Club recognizes 121 breeds of purebred dogs. When ancestors of a pure breed are known and registered by a breed club, the dog is said to have a pedigree.

37. Some people argue that scientific tampering with plants and animals by artificial selection will do more harm than good. Which statement best supports this argument?

    (1) The dog is now human's best friend.
    (2) Many hybrids and pure breeds can no longer survive in the wild.
    (3) There are now 121 breeds of purebred dogs.
    (4) Humans are agents of plant and animal evolution.
    (5) Inbreeding fixes desirable characteristics.

38. A farmer imported several fine long wool Tomney sheep from Australia to breed with his Debouittet sheep, which produce under the difficult conditions on the New Mexico range, in hopes of increasing the value of the flock's wool. This is an example of what?

    (1) pure breeds
    (2) inbreeding
    (3) crossbreeding
    (4) hybridization
    (5) fertilization

Question 39 refers to the following passage.

Tetanus is often a fatal human disease. Sometimes called lockjaw, tetanus is caused by Clostridium tetani bacteria that live in the soil in large numbers. A wound that gets dirt or soil in it is likely to contain these bacteria.

Tetanus bacteria multiply only in the absence of oxygen. Thus, surface wounds exposed to the air rarely allow the bacteria to multiply. Deep wounds, however, are ideal for the development of the disease.

39. Which of the following is a condition that would greatly increase the probability of developing tetanus?

    (1) a bullet wound during a store robbery
    (2) a puncture wound while digging in the garden
    (3) a floor burn while playing basketball
    (4) a hairline fracture to the skull during an auto accident
    (5) a mosquito bite

Question 40 refers to the following diagrams.

Animal Cell

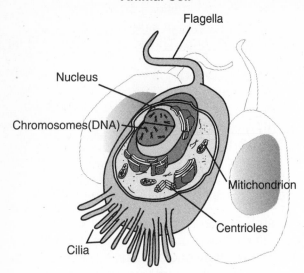

Virus Cell

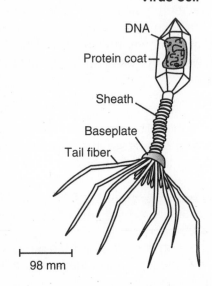

Question 41 refers to the following passage.

The bird called a robin in America is completely different from the bird called a robin in China. Before Carolus Linnaeus devised his universal, Latin-based system for naming organisms in 1735, it was difficult for scientists to communicate accurately about organisms they were studying. Linnaeus's system classified organisms into orderly groups, with part of each organism's scientific name indicating the group to which it belonged. With this system, scientists can distinguish the American robin from the Chinese robin because each has its own particular scientific name, within the group birds. Linnaeus's classification system was a major contribution to the science of biology, and it is still used today.

41. Which of the following is implied by the above passage?

    (1) Scientists could not study organisms prior to 1735.
    (2) An accepted, orderly system aids scientific learning and communication.
    (3) All scientific communication is in Latin.
    (4) The scientific name for humans is Homo sapiens.
    (5) Some organisms in the same group have the same scientific name.

40. Based on the diagrams, which of the following statements best summarizes the difference between the DNA in an animal cell and the DNA in a virus?

    (1) The virus contains more DNA than the animal cell.
    (2) The animal cell contains more DNA than the virus.
    (3) The animal cell contains DNA helpers, but the virus does not.
    (4) The DNA in the animal cell is in a nucleus; the virus has no nucleus.
    (5) Both cells have parts to help them move around.

Question 42 refers to the following diagram.

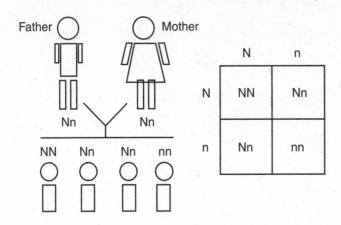

In the above diagram, N stands for the gene for brown eyes, which is a dominant trait, and n stands for the gene for blue eyes, which is a recessive trait. For a recessive trait to be expressed, the offspring must have two genes for that trait.

42. Based on the diagram, what is the likelihood that a child born of these parents will have blue eyes?

    (1)   0 percent
    (2) 25 percent
    (3) 50 percent
    (4) 75 percent
    (5) 100 percent

Question 43 refers to the following information.

Some people say that it is an increase in the sun's energy, and not greenhouse gases, that is causing global warming. In the 1990s, the sun's energy increased in intensity. This means that more of the sun's heat is reaching Earth. These people say that it is incorrect to suggest that emissions of greenhouse gases, such as carbon dioxide, are causing a general warming of the climate. Scientists have shown that the increase in the sun's energy has been responsible for a warming of the global climate of 0.5° Celsius per century. In light of this information, alarmists who say people should stop burning fossil fuels in order to prevent global warming just don't know what they are talking about.

43. Look at the following facts. Which fact demonstrates that the above argument uses faulty logic?

    (1) The sun's rays do not contain a greenhouse gas.
    (2) Fossil fuels are not affected by increased solar energy.
    (3) A warming climate will improve agricultural production.
    (4) The climate is actually warming at the rate of 2.5° Celsius per century.
    (5) Carbon dioxide is not the only greenhouse gas.

Global Malaria Distribution

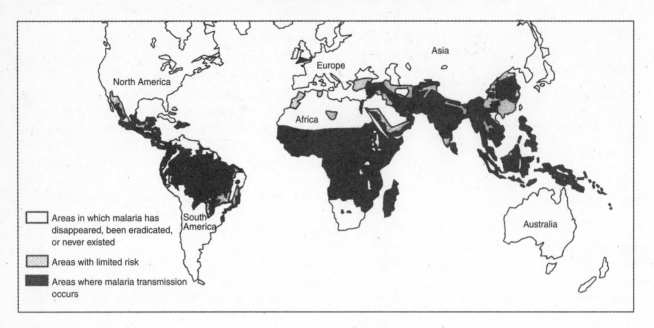

Areas in which malaria has disappeared, been eradicated, or never existed

Areas with limited risk

Areas where malaria transmission occurs

44. Which of the following is a conclusion that can be drawn based on the map above?

(1) In most cases of malaria diagnosed in the United States, the individual contracted the disease outside the U.S. border.

(2) Effective programs have eradicated malaria in Southeast Asia.

(3) Australia is likely to become an area of limited risk for malaria in the near future.

(4) The cold and temperate areas of the world present the greatest risk in contracting malaria.

(5) Malaria is not a serious threat to most of Earth's population.

Question 45 refers to the following information.

Heat flows, or moves from place to place, in three ways.

Conduction—Heat energy is the vibration of atoms or molecules in matter. Heat flows by conduction when rapidly vibrating molecules bump into their neighbors and make them vibrate faster.

Convection—In a fluid, which can be a liquid, a gas, or a flowing mixture, heat often flows by convection. When part of the fluid is heated, it becomes less dense than the surrounding fluid and rises. This movement of the fluid carries heat energy to other parts of the fluid.

Radiation—Heat can be transferred to an object by radiant energy. Radiant energy from the sun passes through space and the atmosphere. When it strikes an object, it makes that object's molecules vibrate faster.

45. You place a pot of water on the heating element of an electric stove. As the water goes from cold to boiling, how is heat flowing?

(1) conduction
(2) convection
(3) conduction and convection
(4) radiation and convection
(5) radiation and conduction

46. There is really no reason people should be concerned with preserving other species. Biodiversity—the presence of many different species of organisms—is just not important to human survival. The dodo became extinct hundreds of years ago. The last passenger pigeon died in 1913. These extinctions had no effect on people.

What is wrong with the above argument?

(1) It does not say that the dodo lived on just one small island.
(2) It does not take what happened to the dinosaurs into account.
(3) It expands its argument from two species to all species.
(4) It does not discuss plants needed for food.
(5) It discusses human life only in terms of economics.

47. In 1907, Ernest Rutherford's assistant conducted an experiment to show how atomic particles pass through a thin sheet of metal. To his amazement, some particles did not pass through the sheet, but bounced off it. The bouncing particles were large and positively charged, so they couldn't be electrons. Rutherford's assistant thought he had made a terrible mistake in the experiment, but Rutherford asked, "What are those bouncing particles?" He and his assistant conducted many more experiments to find out. Eventually, Rutherford discovered the atomic proton.

This is an example of which fundamental principle of scientific inquiry?

(1) Particles having the same charge repel each other.
(2) All experiments must be controlled to get the desired results.
(3) Never let an assistant do your work.
(4) If you are not trained in scientific methods, you make mistakes.
(5) Unexpected results in experiments often lead to new questions and discoveries.

Question 48 refers to the following diagram.

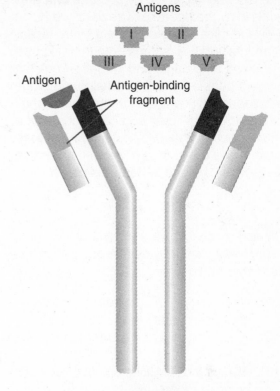

Antibody

An antibody is a cell produced by the immune system to defend the body against disease-causing organisms. Each antibody cell has antigen-binding fragments. The fragments have a specific shape that allows the antibody to attach to and neutralize just one specific type of antigen.

48. In the above diagram, which of the antigens pictured can the antibody neutralize?

(1) I
(2) II
(3) III
(4) IV
(5) V

Question 49 refers to the following passage.

Lyme disease is caused by bacteria that are transmitted by the deer tick. The ticks are found on deer and mice. People contract Lyme disease when an infected tick fastens onto their exposed skin. Wearing long pants and long-sleeved shirts can protect people from deer ticks. Symptoms of Lyme disease include a rash at the spot of the tick bite, followed by fever and headache. If you may have been exposed to ticks and have these symptoms, see a doctor right away. If untreated, Lyme disease can lead to heart disease.

49. Which of the following statements is a conclusion about Lyme disease rather than a supporting detail?

   (1) Untreated, Lyme disease may lead to chronic arthritis.

   (2) A stiff neck may be a symptom of Lyme disease.

   (3) Always look for ticks on your body after being outdoors.

   (4) A rash does not always develop after a tick bite.

   (5) Lyme disease is preventable if precautions are taken.

Question 50 refers to the following passage.

A corporation has created one type of genetically modified potato plant that contains a pesticide in every cell of the plant. The pesticide kills Colorado potato beetles. Short-term studies indicate that lab animals fed only these potatoes had no ill effects. The company assures the public that the genetically modified potatoes are completely safe for human consumption.

50. Why is the above argument inadequate to support the company's claims?

   (1) It does not say how much potato the lab animals ate.

   (2) It does not state which pesticide is in the potatoes.

   (3) It ignores the fact that pesticides kill living things.

   (4) It does not address the long-term effects of eating these potatoes.

   (5) It was written only to help the company sell its products.

SCIENCE

The chart below will help you determine your strengths and weaknesses on the content and skill areas of the GED Science Test. Use the Answer and Explanation Key starting on page 90 to check your answers on the test.

Directions: Circle the number of each item that you answered correctly on the Simulated GED Test A. Count the number of items you answered correctly in each column. Write the amount in the Total Correct space of each column. (For example, if you answered 17 life science items correctly, place the number 17 in the blank before out of 23.) Complete this process for the remaining columns.

Count the number of items you answered correctly in each row. Write that amount in the Total Correct space of each row. (For example, in the Comprehension row, write the number correct in the blank before out of 9.) Complete this process for the remaining rows.

Content / Cognitive Level	Life Science (Unit 1)	Earth and Space Science (Unit 2)	Physical Science (Unit 3)	Total Correct
Comprehension	3, **13, 28**, 29, **40**, 41, **42**		**8, 20**	_____ out of 9
Application	4, **33**, 38, 39	**7, 27**, 32	**10, 11, 12**, 18, **24, 25, 26**, 45	_____ out of 15
Analysis	**5**, 9, 17, **36, 44**, **48**, 49	**1, 31**, 35	2, **19, 21**, 30, **34**, 47	_____ out of 16
Evaluation	**6**, 23, 37, 46, 50	14, **15**, 16, 22, 43		_____ out of 10
Total Correct	_____ out of 23	_____ out of 11	_____ out of 16	Total Correct: _____ out of 50 1–40 = You need more review. 41–50 = Congratulations! You're ready.

(**Boldface** items indicate questions that include graphics.)

If you answered fewer than 41 questions correctly, determine which areas are hardest for you. Use the *Steck-Vaughn GED Science* book and review the content in those specific areas.

In the parentheses beneath the column headings, the unit numbers indicate where you can find specific instruction about that area of science in the *Steck-Vaughn GED Science* book. Also refer to the chart on page 3 of this book.

SCIENCE

Directions

The Science Simulated Test consists of multiple-choice questions intended to measure your understanding of general concepts in science. The questions are based on short readings that often include a graph, chart, or diagram. Study the information given, and then answer the questions that follow. Refer to the information as often as necessary in answering the questions.

You should spend no more than 80 minutes answering the 50 questions on Simulated Test B. Work carefully, but do not spend too much time on any one question. Do not skip any items. Make a reasonable guess when you are not sure of an answer. You will not be penalized for incorrect answers.

When time is up, mark the last item you finished. This will tell you whether you can finish the real GED Test in the time allowed. Then complete the test.

Record your answers to the questions on a copy of the answer sheet on page 110. Be sure that all required information is properly recorded on the answer sheet.

To record your answers, mark the numbered space on the answer sheet that corresponds to the answer you choose for each question on the test.

Example:

Which of the following is the smallest unit in a living thing?

(1) tissue
(2) organ
(3) cell
(4) muscle
(5) capillary

The correct answer is "cell;" therefore, answer space 3 should be marked on the answer sheet.

Do not rest the point of your pencil on the answer sheet while you are considering your answer. Make no stray or unnecessary marks. If you change an answer, erase your first mark completely. Mark only one answer space for each question; multiple answers will be scored as incorrect. Do not fold or crease your answer sheet.

When you finish the test, use the Analysis of Performance Chart on page 89 to determine whether you are ready to take the real GED Test, and, if not, which skill areas need additional review.

Adapted with permission of the American Council on Education.

Directions: Choose the one best answer to each question.

Question 1 refers to the following graph.

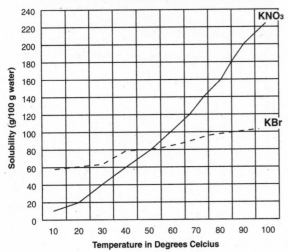

Solubility and Temperature:
Potassium Bromide (KB$_r$) and Potassium Nitrate (KNO$_3$)

Question 3 refers to the following table.

Boiling Point of Water at Various Locations

Location	Boiling Point (°Celsius)
La Paz, Bolivia	91.4
Denver, Colorado	94.0
Madison, Wisconsin	99.0
New York, New York	100.0
Death Valley, California	100.3

3. The higher the altitude, the lower the temperature at which water boils. Which of the following locations listed in the table is at the highest altitude?

   (1) La Paz
   (2) Denver
   (3) Madison
   (4) New York
   (5) Death Valley

1. You conduct a solubility experiment in which the temperature of the solution is 22° Celsius. Using the information in the graph, approximately how much more potassium bromide (KBr) than potassium nitrate (KNO$_3$) can you expect to dissolve in 100 grams of water?

   (1) 20 grams
   (2) 40 grams
   (3) 60 grams
   (4) 80 grams
   (5) 100 grams

Question 4 refers to the following information.

Saturated fat: solid at room temperature; derived from animal products

Polyunsaturated fat: liquid at room temperature; derived from plant products

2. A law of physics states that a body in motion will continue in motion unless acted upon by a force of resistance. The greater the resistance, the more the motion is reduced, and eventually stopped. In which of the following circumstances is resistance to motion the greatest?

   (1) bowling ball rolling down a bowling alley
   (2) tennis ball rolling on a lawn
   (3) leaves blowing in the wind
   (4) boulder rolling downhill
   (5) car rolling on paved road

4. Heart disease is known to be caused by a diet high in saturated fat. If you wanted to eliminate saturated fat from your diet, which of the following would you choose to eat for lunch?

   (1) potatoes fried in lard
   (2) grilled cheese made with butter
   (3) vegetables cooked in olive oil
   (4) chicken fried in corn oil
   (5) grilled steak

Question 5 refers to the following information.

For some people, a single bee sting is a serious matter. Within a number of minutes of being stung, an individual may start wheezing, experience difficulty swallowing, become pale, and eventually collapse. The person should remain calm, minimize activity, and seek medical attention.

5. Which of the following relationships is most like a bee sting to a person who is hypersensitive to bee venom?

    (1) rattlesnake bite to a dog
    (2) cat bite to a mouse
    (3) fish bite to the fish bait
    (4) heart attack to a human
    (5) accident to a driver

Question 6 refers to the following illustration.

6. Each individual in the diagram has his or her right arm pointing upward. Which of the following statements defines up?

    (1) Up means toward the North Pole.
    (2) Down means toward the South Pole.
    (3) Up means east or west.
    (4) Up means away from Earth.
    (5) Down means toward the equator.

Questions 7 and 8 refer to the following diagram.

Levels of Complexity for Lifeforms

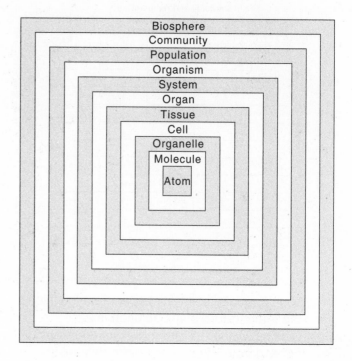

7. Which of the following series is correctly ordered from least to most complex?

    (1) atoms, cells, communities, organs
    (2) molecules, cells, tissues, atoms
    (3) organs, tissues, cells, molecules
    (4) organisms, populations, communities, biosphere
    (5) biosphere, communities, population, organisms

8. Your biology teacher asks you to prepare a report on the most complex living structure among the choices given below. Which do you choose?

    (1) a nerve cell
    (2) the circulatory system
    (3) the liver
    (4) DNA
    (5) hand muscles

Question 9 refers to the following illustration.

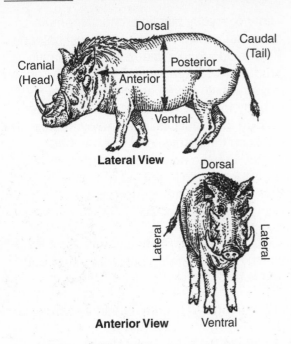

Dorsal

Caudal
(Tail)

Cranial
(Head)

Posterior

Anterior

Ventral

Lateral View

Dorsal

Lateral

Lateral

Anterior View   Ventral

9. What is the fin extending above the
    backbone of a fish <u>most likely</u> to be called?

    (1) a dorsal fin
    (2) a posterior fin
    (3) a caudal fin
    (4) a ventral fin
    (5) a lateral fin

10. Scientists have been able to germinate
    seeds taken from the Egyptian pyramid
    tombs. Which of the following is an
    appropriate conclusion to draw from the
    above statement?

    (1) Plants live longer than animals.
    (2) Animals do not have food storage as
        part of the reproductive process.
    (3) Plant reproduction is superior to animal
        reproduction.
    (4) Animals that hibernate could also be
        preserved for long periods.
    (5) Some seeds are able to survive during
        long periods of dormancy.

Question 11 refers to the following passage.

A basic law of physics is the law of the
conservation of energy. This law states that
energy is neither created nor destroyed. This
means that in a reaction, the energy you start out
with is equal to the energy you end up with, even
if the energy at the end is in a different form.

When you burn a fuel, the chemical reaction
transforms the fuel into heat (and sometimes
into light), into emissions of gases and non-
combustible materials, and into residue. For
example, if you burn a log, heat and light are
produced along with gaseous and particulate
emissions (which go up the chimney), and a
residue—ashes. The amount of energy contained
in the log exactly equals the amount of energy
contained in the heat, light, emissions, and
residue.

11. Based on the law of the conservation of
    energy, in choosing a heating system for
    your house, you would want a clean-burning
    fuel that does which of the following?

    (1) yields abundant energy in the form of
        light
    (2) burns at a low temperature
    (3) transforms most of its energy into heat
    (4) is a gas at room temperature
    (5) yields abundant biodegradable residues

Simulated Test   73

Question 12 refers to the following information and diagram.

In the 1600s, Robert Boyle conducted the experiment shown in the diagram below. In one J-shaped tube, he placed 30 inches of mercury (Hg), with the rest of the tube filled with air. The air in the tube was trapped by a covering on one side of the tube and by the mercury on the other. The second tube contained the same materials. Then, Boyle poured an additional 30 inches of mercury into the second tube. He observed that the air in the tube became compacted—it took up less space. From this result, Boyle formulated Boyle's Law. This law states that for gases, pressure (in this case, the force exerted by the mercury) and volume (amount of space the air takes up) are inversely related. Doubling the pressure on the air halved its volume.

Boyle's Experiment

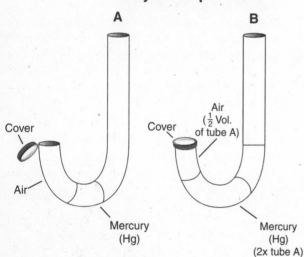

12. Boyle's experiments also provided support for the idea that atoms contain empty space. What in Boyle's experiment supports this idea?

(1) The volume of air in the second tube was compressed.
(2) The volume of air in the first tube remained the same.
(3) Boyle placed additional mercury in the second tube.
(4) The air and mercury took the shape of the J-shaped tube.
(5) The covers on both tubes stayed in place.

Question 13 refers to the following passage.

13. Many everyday plastic products contain a chemical known as PVC (polyvinyl chloride). PVC is added to a wide variety of plastic products to soften them. Recently, European governments have banned the use of PVC in baby toys. Researchers found that the PVC in the plastic is ingested by babies who chew on these toys, and this has been shown to have negative health effects. PVC is also known to leach out of plastic containers and into food when the containers are heated.

To avoid the adverse health effects of PVC, which of the following uses of PVC should you avoid?

(1) putting PVC containers in a microwave oven
(2) using a garden hose containing PVC
(3) buying a basketball containing PVC
(4) wearing sandals containing PVC
(5) using a credit card made from PVC

14. Photosynthesis is the process by which a plant takes in carbon dioxide and, using water and the energy in sunlight, converts it into the sugars it uses to grow and sustain itself. The byproducts of photosynthesis, water and oxygen, are given off by the plant.

What is the purpose of photosynthesis?

(1) to aid plant respiration
(2) to break down proteins for growth
(3) to create food for the plant
(4) to absorb sunlight
(5) to transform sugar into water and oxygen

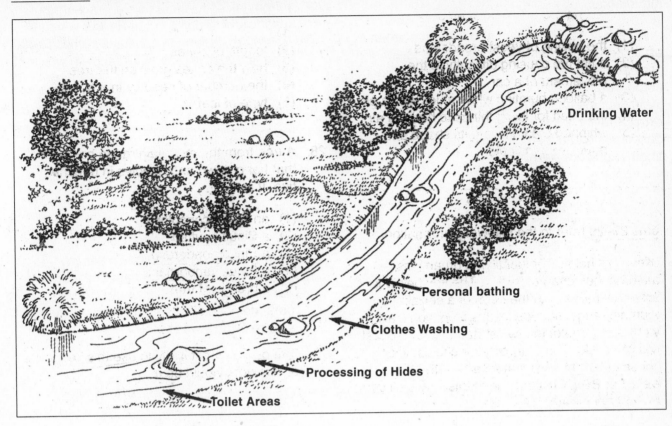

15. A primitive village had strong taboos (restrictions) about the use of a nearby stream. Which change would <u>most likely</u> have the greatest negative effect on the village's water supply?

(1) construction of a government school
(2) a medical outpost established in the village
(3) a dye business assigned to the stream between the processing of hides area and the toilet area
(4) another tribe building a village close by upstream
(5) another tribe building a village close by downstream

Questions 16 through 19 refer to the following information.

A warp is a hole in the matrix of space around an object. The greater the mass of the object, the greater the warp. Whether or not another object in the warp can escape depends on the speed of the object attempting to leave and the size of the warp. <u>Gravity</u> is the word scientists often use to describe the effect on an object caught in another object's warp.

Earth's Warps

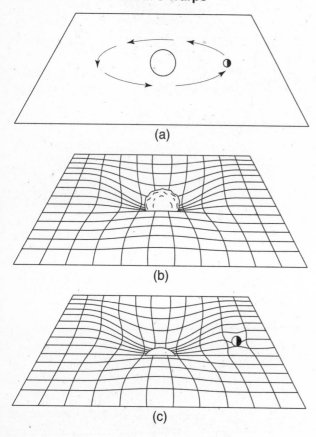

(a)

(b)

(c)

16. What is the reason people do not fall off Earth into space?

    (1) Air pressure pushes objects against Earth.
    (2) Earth's spin on its axis sucks objects to itself.
    (3) Earth's magnetism attracts all objects.
    (4) Objects are caught in the warp created by the mass of Earth.
    (5) People live only on the <u>up</u> side of Earth.

17. The speed of the moon is sufficient to keep it from falling further into Earth's warp but insufficient to pull it out of Earth's warp. Therefore, the moon constantly orbits Earth. A similar explanation would explain which of the following?

Why Earth

    (1) rotates on its axis
    (2) is tilted on its axis
    (3) orbits the sun
    (4) has day and night
    (5) has seasons

18. Energy traveling at 186,000 miles per second is sufficient to escape the warps in our solar system. Which of the following persons need not be concerned with the size of Earth's warp?

    (1) a physicist in charge of the kind and amount of fuel needed for a solar probe
    (2) an astronaut in charge of the flight maneuvers for an exploratory trip to the moon
    (3) a computer analyst in charge of the space shuttle's orbital path and re-entry
    (4) an astronomer on Earth recording radio signals from radiating stars in the Andromeda Galaxy
    (5) an aerospace engineer in charge of putting a communication satellite into orbit

19. The planet Jupiter is 318 times more massive than Earth. What would be required to escape Jupiter's warp?

    (1) the same force as to escape Earth
    (2) a greater force than to escape Earth
    (3) a lesser force than to escape Earth
    (4) finding a hole in the warp
    (5) an object with greater mass than Jupiter

Question 20 refers to the following graph.

Number of Legs of Selected Animal Groups

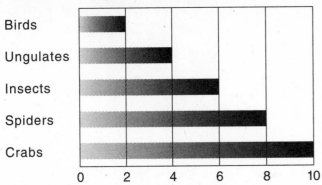

20. Based on the graph, which of the following statements is true?

    (1) All winged animals have six legs.
    (2) Sea creatures usually have more legs than land creatures.
    (3) A characteristic that distinguishes a spider from an insect is the number of legs.
    (4) Crabs have more complex bodies than insects.
    (5) If an animal is not an ungulate (hoofed animal), it cannot have four legs.

Question 21 refers to the following passage.

In an attempt to enhance production of field crops, the state of Maryland established a free soil-testing program through the state university. The state's agricultural extension service then advertised the free program to farmers. Specialists recommended types and amounts of fertilizers needed for maximum production of specific crops based on requested soil analyses. Utilizing the recommendations, farmers increased production, income rose, and the state received increased revenues.

Many farms required yearly applications of chemicals as the rainfall washed the dissolved nutrients into rivers feeding the Chesapeake Bay. Farmers tilled more acreage, loosening additional soil particles that washed into the bay. Plant life in the bay flourished with the increased soil and nutrients, turning large areas into marshland. Algae clogged the waterways, and the excess nutrients upset the chemical balances in the water. This endangered the fish, oyster, and crab populations, and increased the price for bay fish and shellfish. Industries that previously thrived on bay fishing then failed and state revenues declined.

21. Which of the following statements best describes the message of the passage above?

    (1) Using science to solve practical problems is usually ineffective.
    (2) Sometimes the scientific solution for one problem presents another problem.
    (3) The world's food problems will never be solved.
    (4) Farmers should not use fertilizers to enhance food production.
    (5) Farmers should pay for cleaning the Chesapeake Bay since they caused the problems.

Oxidation is the combining of a chemical with oxygen. If oxidation is fast, burning takes place. In burning, heat and sometimes light energy are released, and ashes or exhaust gases are the end result. The fast release of heat or light energy by oxidation is called fire.

22. In the body, food is used as fuel. Oxygen is taken in through the lungs. The blood transports both oxygen and food to the cells where burning takes place. Which body process is evidence that burning is taking place in the body?

(1) growth in size
(2) reproduction
(3) maintenance of body temperature
(4) repair of injured cells
(5) circulation of blood

Receptor cells in the nose respond to gases, while those on the tongue respond only to liquids. The concentration of the chemical in the gas or liquid as well as the time and amount of exposure around the receptor cells determines the intensity of the taste or smell.

Saliva dissolves small amounts of solid foods which then in solution are exposed for taste identification. Solids and liquids can be smelled when molecules on the surface evaporate to become gases.

23. What can a person do to experience the most taste from a liquid?

(1) dilute the liquid
(2) collect extra saliva in the mouth prior to drinking
(3) swallow large quantities quickly
(4) swish or roll the liquid around the tongue prior to swallowing
(5) hold the nose closed while drinking

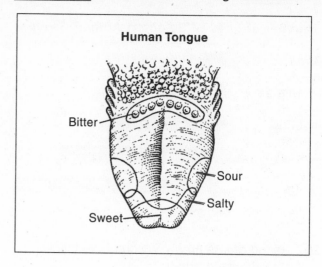

Human Tongue

Bitter

Sour

Salty

Sweet

24. A mother has to give a bitter liquid medicine to her child. What might the mother do to minimize the bitter taste sensation?

(1) place the spoon to the right side of the mouth
(2) place the spoon to the left side of the mouth
(3) place the spoon over the back portion of the tongue
(4) place the spoon just over the tip of the tongue
(5) let the child sip the medicine through a straw

Question 25 refers to the following information.

Keys are helpful for identifying organisms based on their characteristics. The key below is part of a larger key to the trees of a certain mountain range. In a key of this type, you start by choosing one of the two statements at the first level (A or AA). Then, under your choice, you choose one of the two statements at the next level (B or BB). You continue in this way until you arrive at the organism's name.

A. Leaves needle-like (conifers)
  B. Cones hang down
    C. Needles in bunches
      D. Needles in bunches of five—
        Pinus lambertiana
      DD. Needles in bunches of three
        E. Cones greater than 8 inches
          long—Pinus coulteri
        EE. Cones less than 5 inches
          long—Pinus ponderosa
    CC. Needles single—Pseudotauga
      menziesii
  BB. Cones point upwards—Abies concolor
AA. Leaves flattened and broad, not needle-like (broadleaf trees)

25. A tree from the mountain range has cones that hang down and needles in bunches of five. It is which of the following?

(1) Abies concolor
(2) Pinus coulteri
(3) Pinus ponderosa
(4) Pinus lambertiana
(5) broadleaf tree

Question 26 refers to the following passage.

Soil contains rocks and minerals of many kinds and sizes. The sizes vary from boulders, large stones, and gravel to gritty sand, silt, and powdery clay. Silt is composed of particles smaller than sand but larger than clay.

In addition to rocks and minerals, waste products and the remains of dead plants and animals are found in soil. These materials, called humus, increase the fertility of the soil. Topsoil contains much humus; while subsoil usually contains very little.

Geologists classify soils into three basic types: clay, sand, and loam. Soil type is determined by the preponderance of particle size and type. Most soils are mixtures of differing proportions of two or more materials.

Clay soil is mostly clay with a little sand and silt. Although clay soil is soft and powdery when finely ground, it holds much water and becomes sticky when wet. Clay soil can become extremely hard in drought conditions when the particles bind firmly together.

Sandy soil consists mostly of sand with a little clay and silt. Because of the larger particle size of sand grains, water easily drains from sandy soil. Sandy soil is less fertile than other types, since many of the chemicals in any humus present dissolve in water and are flushed from the soil.

Loam soil combines sand, clay, and silt. It drains water better than clays, contains more humus than sand, and is considered excellent for most crops. However, some crops grow best in sandy or clay soil.

26. A backyard gardener would like to include a small watermelon patch in a garden with clay/loam soil. According to the seed package, watermelon plants require higher than average drainage. What would the gardener would probably wish to do to the soil?

(1) increase the proportion of sand
(2) increase the proportion of clay
(3) decrease the proportion of sand
(4) increase the amount of humus significantly
(5) remove several inches of topsoil

Questions 27 and 28 refer to the following passage.

Butterflies and moths are insects that belong to the order Lepidoptera. Both develop through stages of complete metamorphosis. In the butterfly, the pupa is encased in a hardened covering called a chrysalis, while the moth larva spins a strong, but soft, cocoon that surrounds the pupa.

When the adult emerges, more differences distinguish the moth from the butterfly. Moths generally fly at night, while butterflies are active in the daytime. When at rest, butterflies hold their wings vertically, while moths at rest keep their wings horizontal. Moths have a stout abdomen and feathery antennae, while the more slender butterflies have knobbed antennae.

Lepidoptera aid in cross-pollination as they visit flowers to obtain nectar. The apple worm, cabbage worm, tomato horn worm, and corn-ear worm are all larvae of the Lepidoptera. All larvae are voracious eaters. The adults spend most of their stage seeking mates, with egg laying as the end result. Some larva are notorious for their damage to plants. The gypsy moth is a menace to trees in the northeastern states.

The greatest economic value of Lepidoptera is the production of silk by the silkworm, which is not a worm at all but the larva of a small domesticated moth. Silkworms are grown commercially in China and India.

27. A flower seed company would find butterflies most useful in assisting with which of the following?

(1) butterfly reproduction
(2) chrysalis spinning
(3) apple production
(4) flower pollination
(5) worm destruction

28. An insect with beautiful mosaic-patterned wings lands on a leaf and lays her eggs. These later hatch as caterpillars which eat ravenously, grow rapidly, and molt several times. Finally, each caterpillar spins a cocoon and rests. What is the insect?

(1) worm
(2) Hymenoptera
(3) butterfly
(4) moth
(5) either a moth or a butterfly

Question 29 refers to the following information.

There are two types of butane. Both have the formula C_4H_{10}. Normal butane boils at 0°C, while isobutane boils at −12°C. Chemicals such as these, with the same molecular formulas but with different properties, are called isomers.

Normal Butane

Isobutane

29. The difference in the boiling points of normal butane and isobutane is likely due to which of the following?

The different

(1) kinds of elements
(2) formulas
(3) number of hydrogen atoms
(4) number of carbon atoms
(5) arrangement of the atoms

Questions 30 through 32 refer to the following information.

An arrangement of equipment with a swinging rod and attached object is called a pendulum. Sometimes pendulums are paired to work together. An experimenter attached balls of equal mass and size to string of the same thickness in the manner below. Each pendulum was pulled back exactly 30 centimeters and left to swing. The experimenter counted the number of complete swings in one minute. Each ball was pulled back three times with the following results.

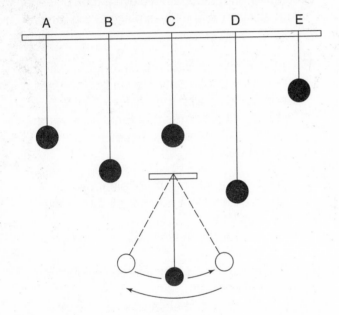

Number of Swings Per Minute of 5 Pendulums

Pendulum	Trial 1	Trial 2	Trial 3	Average
A	22	22	22	22.0
B	10	11	10	10.3
C	21	22	22	21.7
D	8	8	8	8.0
E	44	43	43	43.3

30. What were the factors that were controlled by the experimenter to remain constant during the experiment?

    (1) time only
    (2) time and size only
    (3) time, size, and mass only
    (4) time, size, mass, string thickness, and distance of pull
    (5) time, size, mass, distance of pull, and string length

31. In the hypothesis used by the experimenter to design the experiment, the number of swings was dependent on which of the following?

    (1) the size of the ball
    (2) the mass of the ball
    (3) the length of the string
    (4) the distance of pull
    (5) all of the above

32. What would the result of the experiment lead one to conclude about the number of swings per unit time?

    That the number of swings is

    (1) constant
    (2) dependent on the mass attached to the string
    (3) dependent on the length of the string
    (4) dependent on the thickness of the string
    (5) independent of any factor

Question 33 refers to the following table.

Distribution of Potassium (K) and Sodium (Na) Ions in the Body (mg/100g)

BODY SITE OR CELLS	POTASSIUM	SODIUM
Whole blood	200	160
Cells	20	330
Muscle tissue	250–400	6–160
Nerve tissue	530	312

33. Both potassium and sodium are needed by the body and its cells. Based on the table, which body cells require nearly equal amounts of potassium and sodium?

   (1) red blood cells
   (2) nerve tissue
   (3) muscle tissue
   (4) whole blood
   (5) blood plasma

Question 34 refers to the following passage.

In asexual reproduction, a cell divides through the process of mitosis and becomes two identical cells. During mitosis, the cell's chromosomes, which contain the DNA, are replicated. Each complete set of chromosomes moves to opposite sides of the cell. Then the cell starts to divide. When division is complete, there are two complete "daughter" cells.

34. Which of the following best summarizes the information in the passage?

   (1) Asexual reproduction yields cells with half the normal number of chromosomes.
   (2) Chromosomes have the same charge, and so repel each other.
   (3) Mitosis does not occur in multi-cellular organisms.
   (4) In mitosis, daughter cells have the same DNA as the parent cell.
   (5) Daughter cells are always female.

Question 35 refers to the following passage.

Quantum theory states that at the subatomic level, the motion and the position of a subatomic particle, like an electron, cannot both be determined at the same time. A physicist can measure either one or the other, but not both at the same time. This is due primarily to the electron's being both a wave and a particle. Quantum physics has led physicists to support what they call the "uncertainty principle." Because particle behavior at the subatomic level cannot be known precisely, physicists refer to the "probability" that a subatomic event took place, or that an electron is in a given place at a given time.

35. Albert Einstein was uncomfortable with this quantum uncertainty. He said, "God does not play dice with the universe." This statement indicates that Einstein was most at odds with which aspect of subatomic uncertainty?

   (1) the particle nature of electrons
   (2) the uncertain number of subatomic particles
   (3) the randomness implied by quantum theory
   (4) the lack of sophisticated measuring instruments
   (5) the idea that electrons don't exist

Question 36 refers to the following diagram.

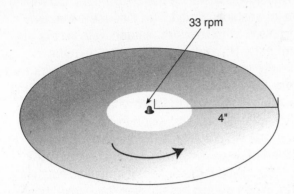

36. In the above diagram, each point along a line drawn from the center of the record to its rim makes a full rotation, or revolution, in the same amount of time. That means that each point on the line has the same rotational, or angular, speed. However, different points along the same line have different linear speeds. A point on the record's rim, for example, must travel a longer distance in one revolution than does a point closer to the record's center.

The angular speed of a point on the record's rim in the diagram is 33 revolutions per minute. The linear speed of a point on the rim equals the angular speed times the radius x 2π. What is the linear speed of a point on the record's rim?

(1) 132.00 inches per minute
(2) 207.24 inches per minute
(3) 264.00 inches per minute
(4) 414.48 inches per minute
(5) 828.96 inches per minute

Question 37 refers to the following information and graph.

This graph is a simplified illustration of the radioactive decay of uranium (U-238) into lead (Pb). In the decay process, particles are given off, changing the uranium atom into a series of different elements, until it becomes stable as the element lead. The bottom axis indicates the number of protons in each atomic nucleus as the atom continues to decay.

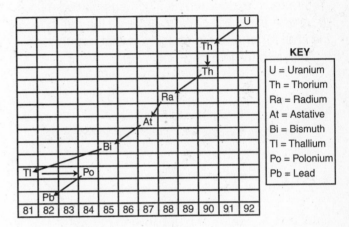

KEY

U = Uranium
Th = Thorium
Ra = Radium
At = Astative
Bi = Bismuth
Tl = Thallium
Po = Polonium
Pb = Lead

37. Based on the graph, how many protons does uranium 238 lose as it decays into its final form as lead?

(1)   6
(2)   8
(3) 10
(4) 18
(5) 22

Question 38 refers to the following information and diagram.

In 1897, J. J. Thomson conducted a series of experiments that eventually led to his discovery of the electron. The diagram shows how Thomson set up a cathode tube with electrodes attached to produce a "cathode ray," or stream of electrons. In experiment A, Thomson shot a stream of electrons right through the tube, from the negative (−) electrode to the positive (+) electrode. In experiment B, Thomson placed a magnet against the cathode tube as the cathode ray shot through it. He observed what happened in each experiment.

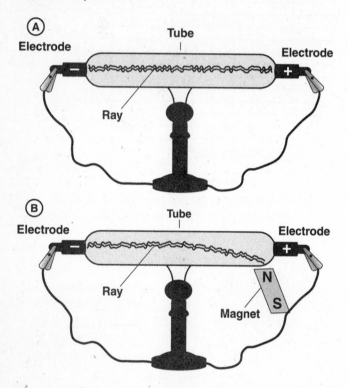

Question 39 refers to the following passage.

Antibiotic resistance results from the pervasive use of antibiotic drugs. The disease-causing organisms antibiotics are intended to kill are quick to mutate. Through mutation, they become immune to the antibiotics that once destroyed them. One major cause of antibiotic resistance in people is eating meat. Factory-farmed animals, such as chickens, are raised in extremely overcrowded conditions. To prevent the rapid spread of disease among them, chickens are routinely given large doses of antibiotics in their feed. When people eat chicken, they take these antibiotics into their bodies. Disease-causing organisms that are resistant to these antibiotics may then make people very ill, or may even kill them.

39. According to the above passage, if you wanted to protect yourself against the dangers of antibiotic resistance, you would do which of the following?

(1) get a flu shot every year
(2) refuse antibiotic injections if you become ill
(3) stop eating chicken from factory farms
(4) make sure the chicken you eat is not diseased
(5) eat only chicken eggs, not chicken meat

38. Which of the following did Thomson discover about the cathode rays from experiment B?

(1) Cathode rays do not originate at the positively charged electrode.
(2) Cathode rays can be bent by a magnetic field.
(3) Magnets have no effect on cathode rays.
(4) Magnetic fields cannot penetrate glass.
(5) Cathode rays always flow toward magnetic north.

Question 40 refers to the following passage.

When tectonic plates on the seafloor move apart, magma from beneath Earth's crust emerges as lava at the seafloor surface. This occurs at sites of seafloor spreading, where new crust is being formed. Scientists have found that the flows of deep-sea lava are aligned on the seabed relative to the magnetism of Earth. For instance, the lines of relatively recent flows are oriented toward magnetic north. This indicates that the lava flows themselves contain magnetized materials. However, scientists have discovered that undersea lava flows from millions of years ago are aligned differently. They all point in the same direction, but it is not the direction of today's magnetic north.

40. Which of the following is a conclusion that can be drawn from the passage, and not simply a detail?

(1) New crust is formed on the sea floor.
(2) Magnetic north has not always been in the same place.
(3) There are volcanoes under the seas.
(4) Undersea lava flows are aligned relative to the magnetism of Earth.
(5) Lava flows contain magnetized materials.

Question 41 refers to the following diagram.

Hydrogen and Two Isotopes

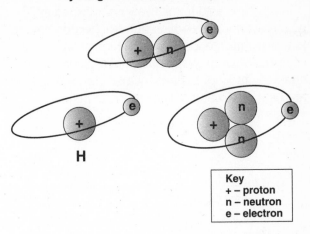

Key
+ – proton
n – neutron
e – electron

41. The illustration above shows an atom of hydrogen and its two isotopes. Based on this diagram, what component of an atom is responsible for the existence of isotopes?

(1) the electron
(2) the quark
(3) the proton
(4) the nucleus
(5) the neutron

42. In Europe, more and more people are choosing to buy only organic food. Organic vegetables are not genetically modified and are grown without the use of agricultural chemicals. Organic dairy products come from animals that are not given antibiotics or hormones, and are provided with organically grown plant-based feed.

Based on this passage, which of the following can you assume is also not part of organic agriculture?

(1) harvesting equipment
(2) pesticides
(3) compost
(4) unfiltered water
(5) fertilizer

Question 43 refers to the following information and table.

In hot, dry regions relatively near the equator, where evaporation is high and freshwater input is low, sea water tends to have a high salinity, or salt content. In warm, wet, equatorial regions, where humidity and input of fresh water from precipitation are high, sea water salinity tends to be low.

AVERAGE SALINITY IN SELECTED BODIES OF WATER	
SEA	SALINITY (ppt*)
Bering Sea	32
Southern Ocean	33
North Sea	35
North Atlantic	36
Arabian Sea	36
Mid-Atlantic Ocean	37
Red Sea	40

*ppt = parts per trillion

43. Which of the seas listed in the table is most likely in the hottest, driest region?

    (1) Bering Sea
    (2) Southern Ocean
    (3) Arabian Sea
    (4) Mid-Atlantic Ocean
    (5) Red Sea

44. In most Western countries today, health care is directed toward individual health needs. Tens of billions of dollars are spent yearly by individuals paying for expensive health care procedures. Yet for only a fraction of that amount, public health measures, such as improved sanitation and free immunization, would do far more to protect and improve the health of the entire population—and health care costs for individuals would go down.

    Based on the above argument, which of the following actions would its author likely support?

    (1) low-cost health care for the needy
    (2) expanded prescription drug coverage for seniors on Medicare
    (3) elimination of free vaccinations for schoolchildren
    (4) stricter standards for drinking water quality
    (5) elimination of cost controls on medical procedures

Question 45 refers to the following passage.

In the U.S. in 1999, West Nile virus, a disease transported to the U.S. from Africa, killed 7 people. The disease was carried by mosquitoes that bred in stagnant fresh water, even in puddles. To maintain public health, it was necessary that the mosquitoes and their developing larvae be killed before they transmitted the disease to more people or animals. In light of this fact, it was irresponsible for some people to protest against the region-wide spraying of malathion, an insecticide. Malathion is known to be effective in killing mosquitoes and their larvae. Though every effort was made to avoid spraying people directly, it was imperative that every part of the affected area receive malathion treatment in case mosquitoes were present. Protesters should have recognized the need for insect control and stopped attempting to alarm the public with stories about the dangers of insecticides.

45. The above argument is inadequate to support its conclusion because it lacks which of the following data?

    (1) the number of birds killed by West Nile virus
    (2) the effectiveness of malathion as compared with DDT in mosquito control
    (3) the fact that only sick and elderly people died from West Nile virus in 1999
    (4) the effects of malathion on human health
    (5) the effects of malathion on controlling mosquitoes carrying malaria

46. Fuel-cell technology uses hydrogen as a source of energy. This process separates hydrogen from a hydrogen-containing compound. The original purpose of the technology was to provide an alternative to fossil fuels, which emit air pollutants when burned. The ideal fuel-cell technology would obtain hydrogen from water, a process which would yield energy without dangerous emissions. However, large automobile manufacturers have taken over much of the fuel-cell research and development. They, along with large oil companies, are developing fuel cells that obtain hydrogen from oil and gasoline. This type of fuel cell would do little to solve the problems of air pollution and global warming.

Which of the following statements could be used to support the conclusion in the above passage?

(1) Oil and gasoline are fossil fuels.
(2) Additives can help gasoline burn more efficiently.
(3) Fuel-cell technology is too expensive for small companies to develop.
(4) Fuel cells can be adapted for home heating.
(5) Hydrogen is difficult to obtain from water.

Question 47 refers to the following passage.

In 1877, when meteorologist Sir Gilbert Walker arrived in India, the monsoon rains failed and famine devastated the country. Walker wanted to know what caused the monsoons to fail every few years and if their failure could be predicted. He began to study world historical climate records. After analyzing decades of records, he noticed a pattern in the variations of air pressure over the oceans. Walker detected a cycle of air-pressure reversals over the tropical Pacific. Every few years, the areas of normal high pressure got low pressure, and vice versa. Walker called the cycle of reversing pressure the "Southern Oscillation." Walker then was able to correlate this oscillating pressure pattern with Indian monsoons. He found that when an unusual area of high pressure moved over the western Pacific, the monsoon rains in India failed. By monitoring air pressure over the ocean, monsoon failure could be predicted and food could be stored to prevent famine. Today, we know that Walker's discovery is related to periodic El Niño's, which scientists refer to as ENSO: El Niño Southern Oscillation.

47. Which of the following describes the method of scientific inquiry Walker used to make his discovery?

(1) data collection over hundreds of years
(2) experimental models
(3) analysis of patterns in historical records
(4) trial and error experimentation
(5) abstract theory

48. Some people question the importance of some species of insects. Yet there are many insect species whose value to the environment is quite evident. For example, without the yucca moth, the yucca plant could not survive. This plant can reproduce only because of the continued survival of one particular species of moth. If that moth became extinct, yucca plants would disappear.

Which of the following is implied in the above passage?

(1) Yucca moths evolved after yucca trees.
(2) We must establish preserves to protect insects.
(3) Insects are valuable as plant pollinators.
(4) Many insect species are becoming extinct.
(5) Yucca moths have no natural predators.

49. Is that canary you have at home related to dinosaurs? Some scientists think it is. New research shows that some dinosaur species nested in large colonies. Females laid eggs, tending them until the young hatched. There is also evidence that dinosaurs may have been warm-blooded. More data are needed, but it appears that there is a closer connection between birds and dinosaurs than was once thought.

Which of the following statements best summarizes the passage?

(1) Dinosaurs and birds have a whole lot in common.
(2) Dinosaurs and birds aren't much alike at all.
(3) Scientists need more data in order to determine exactly how closely related dinosaurs and birds are.
(4) Birds are warm-blooded.
(5) Some scientific evidence points to the possibility that dinosaurs and birds are closely related.

Question 50 refers to the following information and diagram.

This diagram is a simplified illustration of the experiments conducted by Ernest Rutherford in his studies of radioactive rays. Rutherford channeled the radioactive stream of particles emitted by a radioactive substance through an apparatus as seen below. When the radioactive stream emerged, it had been divided into three separate rays.

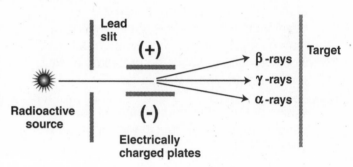

50. Based on this information, what did Rutherford use in his experiment that caused the rays to separate?

(1) the radioactive source material itself
(2) the electrical field
(3) the size of the space between the lead plates
(4) the negative electrode
(5) the target material

SCIENCE

The chart below will help you determine your strengths and weaknesses on the content and skill areas of the GED Science Test. Use the Answer and Explanation Key starting on page 90 to check your answers on the test.

Directions: Circle the number of each item that you answered correctly on the Simulated GED Test B. Count the number of items you answered correctly in each column. Write the amount in the Total Correct space of each column. (For example, if you answered 17 life science items correctly, place the number 17 in the blank before out of 23.) Complete this process for the remaining columns.

Count the number of items you answered correctly in each row. Write that amount in the Total Correct space of each row. (For example, in the Comprehension row, write the number correct in the blank before out of 10.) Complete this process for the remaining rows.

Content / Cognitive Level	Life Science (Unit 1)	Earth and Space Science (Unit 2)	Physical Science (Unit 3)	Total Correct
Comprehension	**6**, 34, 42, 48, 49	14, **16**, 47	**30**, 41	_____ out of 10
Application	4, 5, **8**, **9**, 13, **24**, 25, 27, 39	**17**, **18**, 26	**1**, 2, 11	_____ out of 15
Analysis	**7**, **20**, 23, 28	**15**, **19**, 40, **43**	10, 22, **29**, **31**, **32**, **36**, **37**, **38**	_____ out of 16
Evaluation	**12**, 21, **33**, 44, 45	46	**3**, 35, **50**	_____ out of 9
Total Correct	_____ out of 23	_____ out of 11	_____ out of 16	Total Correct: _____ out of 50 1–40 = You need more review. 41–50 = Congratulations! You're ready.

(**Boldface** items indicate questions that include graphics.)

If you answered fewer than 41 questions correctly, determine which areas are hardest for you. Use the *Steck-Vaughn GED Science* book and review the content in those specific areas.

In the parentheses beneath the column headings, the unit numbers indicate where you can find specific instruction about that area of science in the *Steck-Vaughn GED Science* book. Also refer to the chart on page 3 of this book.

Answers and Explanations

UNIT 1: Life Science

Pages 4–20

1. **(3) chromosome** (Comprehension)
Chromosomes are the only cell structure inside the nucleus. All other structures are found in the cell, but outside the nuclear membrane.

2. **(1) the ability to learn a language** (Comprehension) The ability to learn a language is an inherited trait. Actually speaking a language is, of course, a learned behavior, as are all the behaviors described in the other answer choices.

3. **(5) to regulate the opening and closing of the stomata** (Analysis) The diagram and the passage explain that the guard cells swell or relax to control the size of the stomata. The guard cells have nothing to do with the filtering of light (option 1) or the regulation of temperature (option 4). Plants take in water through their roots, so option 2 is incorrect. Option 3 is wrong because plants take in carbon dioxide and give off oxygen in the process of photosynthesis.

4. **(4) the insulation around electric wire** (Application) The information and diagram explain that the axon is sheathed in a glial cell membrane to keep the electrical signal intact as it is transferred from one neuron to another. In options 1 and 2, the casing is intended to prevent breakage. In options 3 and 5, some heat and light do escape.

5. **(2) natural selection** (Analysis) The passage describes how a change in environmental conditions caused a trait that was less common in the population of English peppered moths to become more common, since it helped the moths survive in the new environment. This is the process of natural selection. Though predation and industrialization are mentioned, they do not explain the process by which dark-colored moths came to outnumber light-colored moths. Neither migration nor hibernation is mentioned in the passage.

6. **(2) bear, dog, beaver** (Comprehension) The tracks of the bear, dog, and beaver are the only ones to show marks beyond the ends of the toes that would be made by toenails.

7. **(2) bear** (Analysis) Bear tracks most resemble human tracks except for the claw prints. Beavers have webbing, hares and dogs have only four toes, and the muskrat toe proportion to foot length is unlike a human's foot.

8. **(3) webbing between the toes** (Application) Webbing between toes is an animal adaptation for swimming, which is necessary for building houses in midstream. The absence of pads or toes and the number and length of toes would not affect the ability to swim.

9. **(4) soft soil** (Application) Long, pointed fingers are good for digging soil. The absence of a grabbing thumb and absence of gripping claws make tree and chimney climbing improbable. No webbing which would be needed for living in midstream is indicated.

10. **(3) Beavers are larger than muskrats.** (Analysis) The beaver track is larger than the muskrat track, so if the tracks are drawn to scale, it is likely that beavers are larger than muskrats. There is no evidence in the illustration to support any of the other statements.

11. **(1) pelts to fur coats** (Application) Pelts (furry animal skins) are processed into fur coats (clothing) in much the same way as hides are processed for leather, except the hairs are not removed. None of the other options indicates an animal skin that becomes clothing.

12. **(1) The skins for leather are a by-product from animals that have already been killed for their meat.** (Evaluation) People who accept the killing of animals for meat do not usually have strong feelings about the hides being used for leather. The use of furs is not recent. Regardless of the reason, animals suffer when killed. Protests are reactions to unnecessary killing, not beauty. The manufacture of footwear does not require leather. Other products such as wood, cloth, and synthetics can be used.

13. **(3) Chemicals used in processing leather cause the allergy.** (Analysis) The allergy is to the chemicals used in processing. The death of the animal or the absence of hair would not cause an allergy. Tanning prevents bacteria from living on the leather.

14. **(2) taking drugs that suppress the patient's immune system** (Analysis) Suppressing the immune system's response would allow the patient's body to accept the organ. Having an organ from a family member would not eliminate the risk of rejection. The options suggesting killing the new organ's cells and injecting the patient with bacteria or viruses do not make sense.

UNIT 1

90   Answers and Explanations

15. **(2) the approximate length of time the trees yield the most fruit** (Analysis) Data from the graph does not consider either oranges or the size of the trees. It shows that peak production of peaches will fall off before that of apples, not the reverse.

16. **(5) wind** (Comprehension) Wind is the only natural agent of pollination mentioned in the passage.

17. **(5) wind** (Application) Plants need no scent, nectar, or petals to attract wind as a pollination agent. Wild plants in nature do not rely on humans.

18. **(1) Male and female flowers grow on separate plants.** (Application) The question implies that two or more plants may make fruit, but one definitely won't. This implication eliminates options 2 and 3. Option 4 is ruled out because human assistance is not what makes the difference between producing and not producing fruit for this plant. Among the remaining options, only 1 describes the only situation in which one plant won't make fruit but two might. Option 5 is ruled out because all fruit-producing plants reproduce by flowers.

19. **(5) produce the reproductive elements necessary for seed formation** (Comprehension) Flowers are the reproductive organs of plants that produce seeds. Providing beauty, nutrition, or indications of plants' nutrient or water needs are not the functions of flowers.

20. **(5) The parent plant is healthy.** (Analysis) A healthy plant is the factor related to healthy seeds. The amount of ovules, size of fruit, and having both male and female structures in the flowers are individual plant characteristics. Pollen reaching the female structure does not insure good health for the seed.

21. **(4) in a commercial greenhouse** (Analysis) Plants in greenhouses do not have access to natural agents of pollination. Nonflowering plants do not need pollination. Farms, deserts, and backyards are accessible to natural agents.

22. **(2) large, white, and fragrant** (Application) A moth is most likely to find a flower that it can both see and smell. Therefore, moth-pollinated flowers are most likely to be white, large, and fragrant. Bright colors aren't useful at night because colors can't be seen in dim light. Moths would be unable to locate odorless flowers. Since moths fly at night, they would not be attracted to day-blooming flowers.

23. **(4) cutting a potato into sections each having at least one eye, and then planting the sections** (Comprehension) New potato plants come from sprouted buds that are located at the eyes. No other option includes the eyes. Potato plants do produce seeds, but they are usually only used to crossbreed to obtain new or improved varieties.

24. **(3) 21.7 grams** (Application) Water is 78.3% of a potato. 78.3% of 100 grams is 78.3 grams. Therefore, removing all the water from a 100-gram potato means removing 78.3 grams of its weight, leaving 21.7 grams.

25. **(3) a hummingbird's long bill** (Application) A giraffe uses its long neck to get food. A hummingbird's long bill is an adaptation that helps it get food from deep bell-shaped flowers. A kangaroo's pouch is a reproductive strategy; a peacock's feathers are a way of attracting a mate. The Arctic hare's white fur and the herding behavior of sheep are adaptations to avoid predators.

26. **(4) DNA** (Comprehension) The scientists are studying the human genome—the genes humans have. DNA is the primary component of genes. None of the other choices refers to the analysis of genes.

27. **(4) Frogs are more susceptible to environmental changes than other organisms.** (Analysis) The passage describes an increase in malformed frogs. Since other organisms in the same areas are not affected in the same way, it can be inferred that the frogs are in some way more susceptible to environmental changes. None of the other options makes sense.

28. **(3) head trauma** (Application) A PET scan is described as a tool used to visualize the brain and brain activity. Of the options offered, only head trauma involves a medical problem related to the brain.

29. **(3) have been tested for safety** (Application) The passage states that an untested protein supplement was associated with the illness and death of many people who took it. Therefore, based on the passage, to avoid harm to yourself, you would want to know if a dietary supplement has been tested for safety. Nothing in the passage indicates that organic supplements or supplements derived from plants are safe. The passage describes over-the-counter supplements, not prescription drugs, and the supplements could work as they are advertised and still have adverse health effects.

30. **(4) Most endangered species' habitats in the wild have been destroyed.** (Evaluation) Even if zoos successfully breed a substantial population of an endangered animal, this population will not survive in the wild if its natural habitat has been destroyed. The remaining options do not identify problems that affect the success of breeding programs.

31. **(3) after A$_2$** (Analysis) The graph shows the greatest increase in antibody production after the injection at time A$_2$. This increase is evident in the more steeply rising graph line, which indicates a greater increase in antibody over a shorter period of time.

32. **(1) stingray** (Analysis) Fish D is a stingray because it is the only fish that is saucer-shaped.

33. **(4) weever fish** (Analysis) Fish B is a weever fish because it is not saucer-shaped. It does not have narrow vertical body stripes. The mouth is not near the bottom of the head. Fish B has a lateral horizontal stripe parallel to the dorsal fin.

34. **(3) C** (Analysis) Fish C's mouth is near the bottom. It has no vertical body stripes and is not saucer-shaped.

35. **(3) dependent on the products and services of camels** (Comprehension) The table indicates that some desert people depend on camels for work, food, clothing, shelter, energy, and transportation. The table does not indicate any threat from camel overpopulation or competition. Eliminating camels would not increase the survival of desert people who are dependent on, not independent of, camels.

36. **(4) food supply is abundant** (Analysis) Since the hump is fat, food must be abundant to make the fat. The hump is not water. The age, pregnancy, or sex of the camel does not affect the amount of fat stored in the hump.

37. **(4) ability to survive in dry climates** (Analysis) Since camels sweat very little, water does not leave the body, thus aiding survival in dry climates. The need for water and salt decreases because they remain in the body. The ability to spit or reproduce is not related to sweating.

38. **(2) prevent sand from entering during sandstorms** (Analysis) Eyelids serve to protect eyes from objects such as sand. Animal eyes are not dry. Eyelids do not affect sleep or sight. Appearing to be blind would not help protect a camel.

39. **(4) Many of today's weeds were the prized plants of colonists.** (Comprehension) Many plants once grown by colonists are now considered weeds. The idea of once a weed, always a weed is not correct. If a plant has a use, it is grown intentionally and not considered a weed. That many weeds were brought from foreign countries is a fact but is not the main idea of the paragraph. Options 3 and 5 do not summarize the paragraph's main idea.

40. **(5) heavy spraying with unregulated chemicals that poison weeds** (Evaluation) Heavy chemical spraying can be unsafe. The methods described in the other options do not pose a possibility of harm to a person eating the food from that crop.

41. **(1) Tt and Tt** (Comprehension) The individual genes shown on the top and left edges of a Punnett square make up the genotypes of each parent. Only option 1 shows these genotypes.

42. **(2) 9** (Analysis) If T is dominant, then any offspring with a T gene will show the dominant trait produced by this gene. The Punnett square shows that the ratio of offspring with the T gene to offspring without it will be 3:1. If there are 12 offspring, the ratio 3:1 becomes 9:3. Only option 2 offers the correct ratio.

43. **(4) half Tt and half tt** (Application) Half of the sex cells of the Tt parent will contain the T gene. Since this is the only source of the T gene, half the offspring will be Tt, and half will be tt. Only option 4 identifies these genotypes.

44. **(3) two sickle cell carriers** (Application) For a child to get two recessive genes, one must come from the father and one from the mother. Therefore, both parents must have at least one copy of the gene. The only couple for which this is true is the couple in which both parents are carriers.

45. **(3) thick, tough skin** (Analysis) Thick, tough skin would keep water from passing in or out. Many leaves would lose water to the air. Spines and thorns are protective devices, not water regulators. Thin skin would allow passage of water. Flower size is not related to water entering or leaving the plant.

46. **(1) the amount of exposure to UV rays that causes skin cancer** (Evaluation) In order to conclude that exposure to sunlight can be controlled to avoid harmful UV rays that cause skin cancer, you need to know the amount of exposure that is considered dangerous. None of the other options—knowing the types of skin cancer that are treatable, other causes of skin cancer, how to apply sunscreen, and the different types of UV rays—helps to support this conclusion.

47. **(2) Sucrose must be broken down before body cells can use the energy.** (Comprehension) The passage states that all sugars are changed to glucose before they are transported to the cells. All other options are incorrect as indicated by the passage.

48. **(3) mannose** (Comprehension) Mannose is a sugar. The names of all sugars end in the letters -ose.

49. **(1) assume the products have no sugar** (Evaluation) Consumers often assume the products have no sugar if the word sugar is not included in the ingredient list. Foods are not usually bought because they have scientific names or lack common names. Excessive intake may cause weight gain.

50. **(4) The microorganisms that digest cellulose do not live in the human digestive system.** (Comprehension) Microorganisms that live in the stomachs of ruminants are not able to survive in the human stomach; thus, humans cannot get energy from cellulose. All other options are untrue or are not supported.

51. **(3) a longer food route** (Analysis) This is the only option supported by the diagram.

52. **(5) careful observation** (Evaluation) The passage describes Darwin's observations and the conclusions he made from them. Trial and error, controlled laboratory experiments, the reproduction of previous field work, and working only with a proven hypothesis are not methods Darwin used in drawing his conclusions.

53. **(4) the measures taken to identify cattle infected before the feed ban** (Evaluation) For the argument that beef is safe to be reasonable, you need to know what measures were taken to identify animals that may be infected but not yet showing symptoms of the disease. Options 1 and 3 do not address the problem. Option 2 still leaves the possibility that animals fed plant food now may have contracted BSE prior to the feed ban. Option 5 has nothing to do with the passage.

54. **(3) pancreas** (Application) The only gland listed in the table that is involved in sugar metabolism and insulin production is the pancreas.

55. **(3) The production of free radicals is controlled by genes.** (Evaluation) Option 3 is the only option that suggests that the two theories of aging work in unison to determine an animal's life span.

56. **(4) Some bacteria are harmful to humans, but others are helpful.** (Comprehension) There are both harmful and helpful bacteria. That bacteria are more beneficial than harmful is an opinion not suggested by the passage. That both plants and animals can get bacterial diseases is a point made by the passage but does not summarize the passage. Bacteria are harmful to humans when bacteria are responsible for disease.

57. **(2) producing insulin needed by diabetics** (Comprehension) Producing insulin is a helpful function of some bacteria. Cabbage rot, salmonella, and anthrax are caused by bacteria, not killed, purified, or cured by bacteria. Bacteria do not poison the pea family but live in plant nodules in a beneficial relationship.

58. **(1) cigarettes to lung cancer** (Analysis) In the example, bacteria to pneumonia show a cause and then a result. None of the other answers shows this relationship.

59. **(5) eight legs and two body sections** (Comprehension) The spider does not meet the two qualifying characteristics of insects because it has eight instead of six legs and only two body segments instead of three. That legs face forward or have joints or that the creature has eyes on top or a big abdomen is not relevant to the qualifying characteristics.

60. **(4) is limited by inheritance but influenced by environmental factors** (Comprehension) An individual's ability to excel at sports is limited by inherited genes but also depends on environmental factors. Options 3 and 5 are incorrect because exercise and food are only environmental factors. Option 1 is wrong because athletic ability is limited by the genetic structure of the human body. Option 2 is incorrect because athletic ability is somewhat determined by the environment.

61. **(3) Is psyllium grown by regular farming methods?** (Evaluation) The method of farming is least important compared to whether the person needs fiber, whether the product may have harmful side effects, whether it is as effective as insoluble fiber, or whether it is needed if other food adjustments can be made.

62. **(4) inability to know that a problem exists** (Evaluation) Elderly people certainly know there is a problem as they are the primary consumers of over-the-counter medications for irregularity. As people age, many bodily functions cease to operate as efficiently. Many elderly persons lack exercise, lack interest in cooking and eating full regular meals, or lack the money to purchase sufficient high-fiber foods.

63. **(3) misinformed** (Evaluation) Misinformed means that a person has not understood an idea correctly. The salesperson could be intelligent, overeducated, interesting, and literate but still have a mistaken idea.

64. **(3) Natural substances are not chemicals.** (Comprehension) The statement that natural substances are not chemicals is false. The salesperson is using this false idea to support a sales pitch. Some chemicals may cause cancer. Both natural chemicals and those changed by humans can be dangerous. Chemicals are sometimes produced in laboratories. These facts, though, are not the false ideas used in this case.

65. **(2) topsoil** (Application) The uppermost layer of soil contains oxygen. In all the other choices, oxygen is either absent, insufficient, or not in the form to support life.

66. **(4) shrimp** (Comprehension) None of the other options are organisms that live in the benthos region.

67. **(5) all ocean animals** (Application) All ocean animals depend on the phytoplankton for food either directly or indirectly. Therefore, all ocean animals would be affected if the phytoplankton died off.

68. **(4) keep kelp near the sunlight** (Analysis) Seaweeds are plants that need sunlight to make food. The sunlight is strongest at the surface. Seaweeds do not swim or need to breathe air. They make their own food and do not trap phytoplankton or animals for food.

69. **(3) is a deep-water fish** (Application) Dark-skinned fish usually live in deep water. The skin color does not determine what a fish eats. River fish are usually light-skinned as rivers are generally not very deep. The question identifies the creature as a fish. How fish are prepared is not dependent on skin color.

70. **(2) fishers** (Evaluation) When fishers wish to catch a particular species of fish, they must know how deep to set their nets. All other options are not people who require knowledge of the depth location of fish for success.

71. **(5) Deep-water fish are often blind or have no eyes.** (Analysis) Fish in deep water do not need eyes, as there is not enough light to see in the dark, deep levels. None of the other options are correct.

UNIT 2: Earth and Space Science

Pages 21–31

1. **(1) CFC-13** (Application) All ODP numbers are based on CFC-11, which has an ODP of 1.0. Therefore, you want to choose a refrigerant that has an ODP number as far below 1.0 as possible. The only choice that has a lower ODP number is CFC-13.

2. **(3) a wall cloud beneath a thundercloud** (Analysis) Tornado funnels develop out of the wall cloud. Option 1 is incorrect because winds at higher elevations must differ from those at lower levels in order for a tornado to form. Option 2 is reversed: the warm air is near the ground, and the cool air is above. Hail and rain do not influence the formation of a tornado, so option 4 is incorrect. Winds in a tornado blow counterclockwise, so option 5 is not correct.

3. **(4) forecasting storms** (Evaluation) Data on cloud size and coverage would be useful in predicting weather patterns, not traffic, pollution, wildfires, or ocean currents.

4. **(2) providing solar-powered cookers and heaters for homes** (Application) The question asks which alternative would save the most forests, therefore the answer must address the activity that most harms the forests. The graph shows that most forest wood is used for heating and cooking.

5. **(3) lava and mudflow deposits** (Analysis) The map indicates the damage done by different volcanic emissions. Though a large area is shown to have been devastated by lateral blast deposits, the question asks for the greatest distance, not the greatest area. The map shows that the rivers adjacent to the volcano carried lava and mudflow farthest from the blast site.

6. **(5) trilobite** (Comprehension) Trilobites are pictured in the lowest layer which was identified in the passage as being the oldest. All other options are in layers above the trilobite.

7. **(5) hard parts of plants and animals** (Analysis) Teeth, shells, wood, and skeletons are the hard parts of plants and animals. Most of the fossils in the drawing are animal parts, but wood is from plants. Trees and dinosaurs with teeth lived on land while starfish, coral, and clams live in saltwater. Clams, starfish, corals, snails, and trees are not extinct.

8. **(2) on the ocean floor** (Analysis) Layer C contains fossils of coral which live in the ocean.

9. **(5) Clams were the first kind of animal to evolve in the oceans.** (Analysis) There are several fossils in the illustration older than the clam fossils, and several of these are of ocean-dwelling organisms; therefore, clams are not likely to have been the first ocean animals. The other statements are all consistent with the evidence in the illustration.

10. **(1) It was covered by the sea for a long time, then became dry land, then was covered by the sea again.** (Application) The oldest four layers of rock have ocean fossils, layer E has land fossils, and the most recent layer, layer F, has ocean fossils. Option 1 is the only statement that matches this evidence.

11. **(4) dry and cool** (Comprehension) Air from central Canada has been primarily over land, at a colder latitude, and so is dry and cool. Wet and humid air develops over oceans, eliminating options 1, 2, and 3. Since Canada is farther north of the equator than the U.S., air from Canada is not usually hotter than air in the U.S.

12. **(3) tropical maritime** (Analysis) Tropical maritime air masses develop near the equator where the increased heat causes great amounts of water to evaporate. To form a hurricane, both heat and water are needed in the air. Polar regions do not contain sufficient heat, and continental regions cannot supply sufficient water for hurricane development. Hurricanes do not develop in cold or dry air masses.

13. **(2) in the uppermost layer of soil** (Comprehension) Earthworms will live where they have the most food, which is the top layer of organic material (decaying plant material is the major form of organic material in soil). The lower layers do not contain organic material.

14. **(4) in a forest** (Analysis) Soil comes from the decay of plants and from the weathering of the parent rock. Therefore, all other things being equal, the deepest soil will be produced where plants grow well and where the parent rock can be easily weathered. This rules out options 1, 3, and 5. In addition, thick soil will not occur where it is likely to erode, such as on a mountainside.

15. **(2) soil with thick layers of organic material and silt and clay** (Application) The passage states that the upper layers contain most of a soil's nutrients, and the diagram shows plant roots growing through both of these layers. Therefore, a soil with thick layers of both organic material and clay and silt is likely to be the most fertile.

16. **(1) Indiana was once covered by an ocean.** (Analysis) If limestone is found, consisting of dead sea creatures, an ocean must have covered that area. A tidal wave brings surface water on land, not ocean bottom rock or soil. Although rivers flow underground, the oceans do not extend underground to the middle of continents. Limestone does not come from desert areas. By definition, fish or sea creatures live in water with only brief stays on land.

17. **(4) The sand that formed the rock was blown there from different places.** (Application) Layers in sedimentary rock are always the result of different sediments gathering in layers before the rock formed. Knowing that wind can carry sand from place to place, it is reasonable to assume that over time, winds carried and deposited different colors of sand to the place where the rock later formed.

18. **(3) sandblasting with air guns** (Analysis) Sandstone is cleaned by air guns that remove the outside particles. Because sandstone is so absorbent, liquids cannot be used to clean it. Paint, water, and varnish would seep into the rock. Wallpaper is not for exteriors.

19. **(5) plastic** (Application) All the other options are made from cement or glass, which require limestone rock.

20. **(3) a three-inch rise in the level of the oceans over several decades caused by partial melting of the polar ice caps** (Evaluation) Because global warming is global and long-term, the local or short-term evidence described in options 1, 2, 4, and 5 cannot be convincing. The polar ice caps could melt only if global warming were occurring.

21. **(4) contain different minerals and impurities** (Application) The color of a gem depends on the mineral of which it is composed and the impurities in the mineral. The scarcity, value, hardness, or gem quality of a stone does not affect its color.

22. **(3) elevation** (Application) Since air pressure changes with elevation, measurements of air pressure could be converted to measurements of elevation.

23. **(2) The pressure of the atmospheric air increases as the elevation decreases.** (Analysis) When the air column is greater, the weight of air pushing on the balloon is greater. Since the balloon and the air inside can expand or contract, the balloon becomes smaller because the air pushes in on each square inch of surface with greater pressure.

24. **(2) Deep sea divers must wear pressurized suits to maintain breathing and to prevent eardrums from bursting inward.** (Application) None of the other options contain an item that can expand or flex in response to increased or decreased pressure.

25. **(3) Copper and iron come from rock materials.** (Analysis) By definition, metals come from ores, which are rocks. Since copper and iron are metals, they must originate in rock materials. All other options may or may not be true but cannot be derived from the information given.

26. **(5) The water cools the air above it, causing the air to sink.** (Comprehension) The land absorbs more energy than the water. The drawing indicates that air is rising over the sand but not over the water. Thus the sand is hotter, has a higher temperature, and causes an inland breeze. The cooler water causes the air to sink.

27. **(4) C and D** (Comprehension) California has the greatest number of quakes, and Colorado has no high-intensity quakes. Hawaii, an island, does have many quakes. New York, on the East Coast, had 52.

28. **(5) Washington** (Analysis) Washington has the highest (1:14). To find the proportion, the number of high-intensity quakes is divided into the total number of earthquakes. California has 1 in 28, Colorado has 0 in 59. North Dakota has 0 in 0, and Utah has 1 in 34.

29. **(1) in, near, or bordering the Pacific Ocean** (Analysis) The states that are in or border the Pacific Ocean have the most quakes: California, Alaska, Hawaii, and Washington. No southern, Gulf, or Great Lakes states are listed. North Dakota, a Great Plains state, has no quakes. The eastern states listed have many fewer quakes.

30. **(2) topaz ring** (Application) According to the table, topaz is the hardest material (after diamond, which is not an answer option) that is also much harder than glass.

31. **(4) crop** (Application) The question asks you to identify the land type showing the greatest overall loss. This is cropland, which declined by about 32 million acres.

32. **(2) continental crust** (Analysis) The diagram shows that the uplifting of land that is forming the mountain ranges comes from continental crust. Both tectonic plates meet at the surface at their uppermost level of continental crust. Though the other, deeper layers of each plate are involved in the collision, only the topmost, crust layer is shown to form mountains.

33. **(3) comparing data over time** (Evaluation) The passage describes scientists comparing data of current atmospheric conditions with data that reflects past conditions.

34. **(3) Vegetation on land absorbs a lot of rain water, thus limiting runoff.** (Analysis) The graph indicates that after a clearcut, during which all or most vegetation is removed, rainwater runoff increases dramatically. As vegetation grows back, rainwater runoff decreases and begins returning to normal. It can therefore be concluded that vegetation living on the land reduces rainwater runoff. Option 3 is the only option that provides a viable explanation.

35. **(4) cooler and wetter winter weather in the Southeast** (Application) The map indicates expected El Niño weather patterns for December to February—winter in the United States. Thus, the correct answer must address winter weather. The map shows that the Northeast and the Northwest will experience warm winter weather, but these are not options. The only option indicated on the map is the swath of wet, cool weather in the U.S. Southeast.

36. **(2) wind** (Comprehension) Winds and sand cause desert dunes. In deserts, the sand is already mostly on the ground, eliminating gravity. Glaciers are not in the tropics. Deserts do not have ocean waves or much running water to cause the huge dunes inland.

37. **(3) dissolves in rainwater and is carried by rivers to the oceans** (Analysis) Salt mines are inland, not on ocean bottoms. At ordinary air temperatures, salt does not evaporate. Salt is a mineral from rocks, not a product of animals. Salt is not a waste of sufficient quantity to cause the salinity of the oceans.

38. **(3) June 21** (Analysis) The longest daylight is in summer. June 21 is the only summer date listed. January and December have short days and March 21 is spring equinox, with equal day and night hours.

UNIT 2

39. **(2) burning fuels** (Application) Cars, trucks, and planes all burn fuels to obtain the energy needed to move. Some researchers have attempted to outfit moving vehicles with solar cells. Nuclear, geothermal, and tidal energy still require a large facility, are restricted to a particular place, or require wires to transmit the energy as electricity.

40. **(2) fossil fuels** (Comprehension) Fossil fuels are made from the materials of organisms that lived in the past. All other options have an accessible energy supply for many future generations to use.

41. **(3) Each year a person's birthday would fall on the same day of the week.** (Comprehension) None of the other options is characteristic of the calendar.

42. **(4) length of a year** (Analysis) The rotation of Earth determines the length of a day (24 hours), and the revolution of Earth around the sun determines the length of a year (a little over 365 days). All the options except option 4 list things that humans have decided and that could be different.

43. **(4) because 365 divided by 13 has a remainder of 1** (Analysis) If a year is divided into 13 equal months, one day is left over. This day is accounted for by "year day."

UNIT 3: Physical Science

Pages 32–49

1. **(3) It has a greater density than the larger object.** (Analysis) The scale is in balance, indicating that both objects have the same mass. Since they obviously differ in size, the smaller object must be more dense—must have more mass for a given volume—than the larger object. Hardness and the placement of the center of gravity do not account for differences in density. Weight is a measurement of the pull of gravity on an object, and inertia is dependent on an object's mass.

2. **(2) oxidation** (Analysis) A chemical reaction in which an oxide forms is called oxidation. Polymerization describes a reaction involving many identical molecules. Fermentation is the process by which complex organic compounds are split into simpler substances. Evaporation is the process in which a liquid changes to a gas. Convection describes one way heat moves.

3. **(2) shaving cream** (Application) Shaving cream is the only option that fits the definition of a colloid, as a permanent mixture of substances that cannot be separated out with a paper filter. Though the bubbles in carbonated soda cannot be filtered out, they eventually leave the liquid. Mud in water settles out, soap bubbles in water burst and disappear, and air in a balloon escapes if the balloon is opened. None of these has the characteristics of a colloid.

4. **(2) hydrogen and carbon** (Analysis) Though some of the compounds are shown to contain oxygen, and one even has nitrogen, there are only two elements that all of these organic compounds contain—hydrogen and carbon.

5. **(3) There are the same number of helium and oxygen molecules.** (Application) Avogadro's Law states that under identical conditions, equal volumes of gases contain an equal volume of molecules. Therefore, there will not be more helium molecules or more oxygen molecules. The number of atoms is not mentioned as part of the law.

6. **(4) Experiments and results must be reproducible.** (Evaluation) The passage describes the events that led to world scientists' rejecting the claim that cold fusion had been accomplished. The reason given for the rejection is that the same results could not be duplicated when an experiment identical to the original was conducted. Only option 4 refers to this requirement of scientific inquiry. There is no indication that the original experiment was not well observed, nor that data were not collected, so options 1 and 3 are incorrect. It is contrary to the scientific method to say that a working hypothesis must be correct—experiments may as easily prove the hypothesis wrong as prove it right. Thus, option 2 is wrong. Option 5 restates a fact but does not address scientific inquiry.

7. **(1) ebony only** (Comprehension) Ebony is the only wood with a density greater than water. Therefore ebony would sink in water, while all the others are less than 1 gm/cm³ and would float.

8. **(1) carpenter** (Evaluation) A carpenter considers a wood's strength and durability when selecting it for a specific task. The other persons do not normally use wood in their work.

9. **(1) pound** (Application) Weight is directly dependent on density. All other prices would not be affected by density; thus the price for all other options would be the same for any wood type.

10. **(3) of 0.6 gm/cm³ or greater** (Analysis) Pine has a density of up to 0.6 g/cm³, so the definitions in options 1 and 2 would include some pine wood as hardwood. The definition in option 4 excludes some hickory, oak, and maple from the hardwood category. Option 5 doesn't make sense if there are only two categories of wood. The definition in option 3 is the best choice since 0.6 g/cm³ is the dividing line between the densest pine and the least-dense hardwoods.

11. **(1) Heat shield tiles get hot during the re-entry of the space shuttle craft.** (Analysis) When a spacecraft re-enters the atmosphere, the craft rubs against the molecules in air, causing heat from friction. Airplanes cannot fly in outer space. The other options are true but do not support the fact that Earth's atmosphere contains matter.

12. **(2) The temperature of the heated liquid is being measured.** (Comprehension) The presence of the thermometer indicates temperature is being measured. According to what is shown in the diagram, all other answers are incorrect.

13. **(1) power lawn mowers** (Application) Of the machines listed, this is the only one that requires oxygen to burn the fuel that powers its parts. All the other choices use electricity.

14. **(1) rocket ships** (Application) Rocket ships have no pistons, wheels, or turbines that assist in movement as the other options have. The entire body, except for the area that releases the gases, is pushed from the inside.

15. **(2) wheelbarrow** (Application) In a wheelbarrow, a force is applied on the handles, the force is transmitted to the load, and the whole thing pivots on the wheel, thus meeting the definition of a lever.

16. **(2) a police car approaches with its siren on** (Application) The passage states that pitch gets higher as a sound approaches a person. Either the person hearing the sound or the source of the sound must be in motion for the Doppler effect to occur, so options 1 and 5 are incorrect. In option 3, the source of the sound and the person hearing the sound are moving together. Option 4 is incorrect because the pitch would get lower as the sound source moves away.

17. **(4) when it is heated to extreme temperatures** (Comprehension) The passage says matter on the sun exists as plasma, but not that the sun is the only place plasma can exist. It says that solids, liquids, and gases can all enter the plasma state at certain temperatures. It says nothing about radiation or pressure.

18. **(5) in glowing stars** (Comprehension) All glowing stars, of which the sun is one, are undergoing nuclear fusion that produces intense quantities of heat energy that ionizes matter into the plasma state. No other options involve heat in the tens of thousands of degrees Celsius.

19. **(2) an ice cube** (Comprehension) When water is frozen it is in a solid state. The other choices are in either liquid or gaseous states.

20. **(1) The energy stored in the steam was transferred to the movable turbine wheels creating motion, and the decrease in energy changed the steam to water.** (Comprehension) Heat energy (stored in the motion of gas molecules) is transferred into the motion of the blades. Having lost heat, the gas returns to the lower energy state of a liquid. The steam acts on the turbine, causing it to respond by turning. The loss of energy occurs whether or not the turbine becomes warm. The blades, in moving contact with the steam, would increase the temperature. Evaporating liquids would decrease the temperature.

21. **(3) CCl₄** (Comprehension) The prefix tetra- refers to the number 4. The letter symbols for carbon and chlorine are C and Cl. Options 1 and 2 do not include the number 4. Co and Cu refer to cobalt and copper.

22. **(1) carbon dioxide** (Comprehension) The subscript 2 indicates two atoms of oxygen. The prefix for the number 2 is di-. There is no other number to indicate the other prefixes.

23. **(1) CH₄** (Comprehension) CH_4 contains only carbon and hydrogen atoms, which is consistent with the definition of a hydrocarbon. All other options contain oxygen.

24. **(3) The melting and freezing temperatures are the same.** (Comprehension) Melting and freezing occur at the same temperature, as shown in the diagram. They are simply phase changes in different directions. The other options indicate differences in temperature.

25. **(1) stays the same throughout the time the water is boiling** (Analysis) The flat line at the boiling temperature in the phase diagram indicates that the temperature of the liquid water stays the same during boiling, even as more heat is added. The other options indicate differences in temperatures.

26. **(3) sorting** (Application) The series of sieves is a mechanical means of sorting fragments by size. All other options are wrong by their definitions.

27. **(2) distillation** (Application) Distillation requires vaporization and condensation for separation. In this way, petroleum is separated to obtain the desired substances. All other options are wrong by their definition.

28. **(4) magnetic separation** (Application) Iron is magnetic and is separated by using magnets. All other options are wrong by their definition.

29. **(1) salt from sea water** (Application) Salt is a solid dissolved in a liquid. The other options don't list solids dissolved in liquids.

30. **(5) There is no experimental verification of absolute zero.** (Evaluation) The passage states that scientists have been unable to achieve absolute zero in a laboratory setting. There is no indication of a disagreement among scientists as to what the correct temperature of absolute zero is, that thermometers are inaccurate, or that the scientists' hypothesis is faulty. The passage states any act of measurement changes the temperature of the system.

31. **(5) wool** (Comprehension) Wool ignites at 400°F. According to the graph, all other required temperatures are higher.

32. **(3) rayon** (Comprehension) According to the graph, silk's kindling temperature is about 1050°F, and rayon's is about half that, or 525°F. No other option satisfies this requirement.

33. **(2) a long-sleeved nylon shirt** (Evaluation) According to the diagram, nylon catches fire only at very high temperatures. A long-sleeved shirt offers more protection than a short-sleeved one.

34. **(4) the blanket prevents the burning item from reacting with the oxygen in the air** (Analysis) When wrapped around a burning object, a wool blanket prevents oxygen from continuing to react with the burning object. That wool has a low kindling temperature or is rough to the touch does not explain how it can be used to put out fire. Water to put out fire must be on the fire and not absorbed by the blanket.

35. **(5) Atoms are mostly empty space.** (Comprehension) The fact that most of the alpha particles passed straight through the gold foil without being deflected shows that atoms are, in fact, mostly empty space. If, as previously believed, atoms were solid spheres, most of the alpha particles would have been deflected by the atoms in the gold foil.

36. **(1) escaped into space** (Comprehension) According to the passage, hydrogen is light; light atoms escape into space. It also says that large amounts of hydrogen were released into the original atmosphere, and that at present, very little hydrogen is in the atmosphere. Therefore, it is strongly implied that the original hydrogen escaped into space. The passage does not mention or imply options 2 or 5.

37. **(2) Hydrogen atoms float in the air and escape into outer space.** (Comprehension) Hydrogen atoms escape into outer space. The fact that water, fuels, fats, and carbohydrates contain hydrogen does not explain hydrogen's absence from air. Hydrogen's presence on the sun and stars does not explain its low concentration in Earth's atmosphere.

38. **(1) one of the atmosphere's heavier elements** (Analysis) Nitrogen sinks in air to Earth's surface because it is heavier than the gases which float. Nitrogen's reactiveness, absence from soil, and its use in life forms do not explain why it sinks.

39. **(5) buzz saws for cutting timber** (Application) A buzz saw's movement to cut wood is not dependent on moving air but is dependent on burning a fuel. All other options require air to function.

40. **(3) Photovoltaic cells have some advantages over fossil-fuel-burning power plants.** (Evaluation) All the conclusions except option 3 require making assumptions or value judgments that don't relate directly to the information in the paragraph.

41. **(5) makes water molecules at the surface more likely to break away from the rest** (Analysis) Evaporation occurs when the molecules of a liquid break away from the surface of the liquid and enter the gas phase. Heating encourages this process because it gives the molecules of the liquid more kinetic energy, which makes them vibrate and move around faster. Heating water does not split its molecules, encourage bonding, or strip electrons.

42. **(4) residual radioactivity** (Analysis) Survivors would need to prevent exposure to the falling particles. All other options are in the past in the first hour after an explosion. Survivors need only be concerned about what is yet to come.

43. **(2) flash** (Comprehension) Flash is an extremely bright light given off at the release of energy and causes blindness. All other options vaporize, break apart, kill, or in some other way affect other body processes.

44. **(4) experiments that detect proton decay** (Evaluation) The author of the passage questions the validity of superstring theories because they have not been confirmed through experimentation. The passage states that experimental evidence of proton decay would lend credibility to the theories. Options 1 and 3 refer to additional dimensions, while option 2 refers to experiments with gravity. Option 5 refers to experiments that show that proton decay does not occur.

45. **(2) the force with which the ball is thrown** (Analysis) The information shows that gravity acts on each ball equally. The only difference in each case is the force of the throw, which changes the speed at which the ball moves. The harder the ball is thrown, the greater the outward distance it moves in 1 second.

46. **(2) ammonia** (Application) Vinegar is acetic acid, with a pH of about 3.0, so you must use a base—a substance with a pH of more than 7.0—to neutralize it. The only basic substance that is an option is ammonia, which is shown to have a pH of about 12.0.

47. **(5) ti** (Application) To sing a note with a higher pitch than <u>la</u>, you must sing one whose frequency, as shown on the chart in Hertz (Hz), is greater than the frequency of <u>la</u>. The only option that is correct is <u>ti</u>, with 495 Hz, higher than <u>la</u>'s 440 Hz.

48. **(5) 1,470 meters per second** (Comprehension) A sonic boom in water must be produced by a sound source traveling at a speed greater than the speed of sound in water, which is 1,469 meters per second. Therefore, a sound source must be moving at a minimum of 1,470 mps to create a sonic boom.

49. **(4) movement of mercury in a thermometer** (Application) A thermometer is the only case listed in which temperature causes a substance to expand or contract. In a thermometer, heating causes the mercury to rise, or expand, in the thermometer tube; cooling causes it to fall, or contract.

50. **(4) 10 cm^3** (Comprehension) The graph shows that there is a 10 percent change in volume from 25° to 55°. Ten percent of 100 cm^3 is 10 cm^3.

51. **(1) Expansion by heat is dependent on the kind of liquid but independent of the kind of gas.** (Analysis) The rate of expansion of liquids depends on the type of liquid. Air is a mixture, but the other gases are not mixtures. The three gases were tested separately but yielded the same results as all three responded in accordance to Charles's Law. Water at 55°C increased to 4 cm^3; whereas petroleum at 55°C changed only to 3 cm^3. Both gases and liquids expand as temperature increases. Liquid expansion is individual, but gas expansion is the same for all gases.

52. **(4) The gases would expand in conformance to Charles's Law.** (Application) Gases from anywhere in the universe are expected to conform to the laws of nature. The origin of the gas and the conditions where it is found should not affect its conformance to universal laws.

53. **(4) increase by an unknown amount** (Analysis) All the lines on the graph show increases, so it can be inferred that the volume of a liquid increases when heated. It is impossible to know how much the increase will be without knowing exactly what the liquid is.

54. **(2) the centripetal force, which pulls rotating objects inward toward a center** (Analysis) The information explains that the force acting on the clothes is one that orients them toward the center of the tub: this is a centripetal force. The small holes allow the water to avoid being acted on by the centripetal force, which is why the water leaves the clothes.

55. **(5) Rats fed large amounts of the compound showed no ill effects over several generations.** (Evaluation) Option 5 describes the kind of evidence that may help convince scientists of a compound's safety. The evidence in option 4 is less convincing because the compound could have long-term effects that don't show up immediately. Options 1, 2, and 3 are irrelevant because even if they are true, the compound could still be harmful.

56. **(4) $357** (Application) If the refrigerator is open 1 hour per day, it uses 7 kilowatts of electricity per day, at a cost of 98 cents (7 x .14 = .98). In one year (365 days) you therefore spend $.98 x 365, or $357 on electricity.

57. **(1) an air pump getting hotter as it inflates a football** (Application) Molecules of air in a pump are under pressure. The more you pump, the greater the pressure on the molecules. The pump gets hot because of the heat resulting from the compression of air. Option 3 involves convection, options 2 and 4 do not involve heat, and in option 5 heat is produced by friction, not compression.

58. **(2) B** (Application) Brakes provide the force needed to stop the motion of the car. All other options are not an attempt to slow or stop an object in motion.

59. **(1) A** (Application) The heavy truck requires more force to change its motion, using more gasoline than the car with lesser mass.

60. **(3) C and D** (Application) Both the boat and the spinner react in the opposite direction to the action. All other options are not responding by movement in the opposite direction.

61. **(2) Earth continues to revolve around the sun.** (Analysis) Example B illustrates part of the First Law, that an object will stay in motion unless a force acts on it. Option 2 is the only example illustrating the continuing motion of an object or the force required to stop its motion.

62. **(1) brass** (Application) Tubas and trumpets are made of metal, have valves to change the length of a vibrating air column, and are brass instruments. They do not have tight skins, reeds, strings, or holes to cover. All instruments must cause vibrations to produce sound. Vibrator is not an instrument group.

63. **(4) strings** (Application) Guitars and banjos have strings that vibrate. Folk is not an instrument group. Guitars and banjos do not have valves, tight skins, or holes to cover.

64. **(3) the gong** (Comprehension) A gong is a percussion instrument made of metal and must itself vibrate to produce sound.

65. **(5) will not change** (Comprehension) If a number is a constant, it does not change. All other options indicate possible change.

66. **(2) The concentration depends on the amount of acid.** (Analysis) Concentration is a dependent variable that changes as the amount of acid varies. Because the concentration was lessened, it cannot be a constant. The amount of acid is of concern to the question, not the amount of solution. A small amount of concentrated acid would not necessarily make a concentrated solution. The concentration was decreased, indicating a relationship to the acid.

67. **(4) is dependent on the surface area exposed** (Analysis) The amount of water left is dependent on the amount of water evaporated, which depends on the amount of surface area exposed.

68. **(3) 1.17 g/cm^3** (Analysis) The plastic is floating on top of the glycerol, which has a density of 1.26 g/cm^3—so plastic must have a density less than this. The layer on top of the plastic, water, has a density of 1.00, so the plastic must have a density greater than this. The only option within this range—between 1.0 and 1.26 is 1.17 g/cm^3.

69. **(2) induction coil** (Comprehension) A van or bus has an induction coil, as do cars and trucks, to change low voltage direct current to high voltage. Batteries supply only low voltage current. Transformers are designed for alternating current.

70. **(5) step-down transformer** (Application) U.S. appliances are made for 120 voltage; when using appliances in countries with 240 voltage, a step-down transformer must be connected between the outlet and the appliance. Batteries and dry cells do not change voltage. Induction coils are used only with batteries. A step-up transformer would increase the voltage.

71. **(3) the flow of electrons is not continuous with static electricity** (Comprehension) Use of electricity depends on a continuous supply that static electricity cannot maintain. Static discharge or continuous flow is not dangerous when protected by fuses. The rubbing just builds up a charge and does not supply a constant flow.

72. **(1) gold and silver** (Application) Gold and silver are used because they are the most durable. All other options are metals that are more likely to burn or need repair.

73. **(4) the contractors who repair the damage or demolish the structure and rebuild a new home** (Evaluation) The contractors make money on fires started by improper fuse installation or usage. All other options result in harm or additional expense to those involved.

74. **(5) aldehyde, carbonyl, and carboxyl** (Analysis) Those diagrams that contain double lines indicate a double bond. Hydroxyl and ether have only single bonds.

SIMULATED TEST A

Pages 51–68

1. **(2) 2.3** (Analysis) Find the year 1950 along the bottom axis and then see that the graph line crosses at 13.5, which the left axis tells you is the sea ice extent in millions of square kilometers. Do the same for the year 1995 to get approximately 11.2. To find the difference between the two, subtract 11.2 from 13.5. This is the amount of ice lost.

2. **(5) lenses** (Analysis) Lenses focus light in glasses to help people see objects more clearly. Mirrors would keep light out. Prisms would produce rainbows of light which would interfere with vision.

3. **(5) Fish size is correlated with maturity and reproductive age.** (Comprehension) The information states that if undersized fish are caught, there will be too few reproducing adults to sustain the population. Therefore, the passage implies that size is directly related to maturity and reproductive age.

4. **(5) annual and hardy** (Application) The information states that the coleus can live through late fall—a cold period. It also says that it must be planted anew each spring. Therefore, its categories are annual and hardy.

5. **(3) size** (Analysis) The animals shown do not eat others that are larger than themselves. All other characteristics vary on the chain.

6. **(3) The top animal has fewer predators.** (Evaluation) The top animal is less likely to be eaten because there are no animals above it on the chain. Being easily seen is not an advantage. Not all animals at the top of a food chain can fly. An advantage for the bottom animal is not necessarily useful for the animal at the top.

7. **(1) restricting significantly the number of animals grazing on range land** (Application) The pie graph shows that the greatest percentage of desertification comes from overgrazing. The other answer choices do not address overgrazing.

8. **(1) 1 to 1** (Comprehension) In a chemical reaction, the number of molecules of each substance involved is indicated by a number written before the molecule. The numbers below the line indicate the number of atoms of each element within the molecule. Since no numbers occur before each molecular formula in this reaction, the ratio of the molecules is 1 to 1.

9. **(3) Sedimentary rock on Mars forms in the same way that sedimentary rock forms on Earth.** (Analysis) The passage states that what appears to be sedimentary rock has been seen on Mars. As no one has studied it closely, it may not be. To suggest that the presence of sedimentary rock proves that Mars has or had water is to make the assumption that sedimentary rock forms the same way on Mars as it does on Earth.

10. **(3) C** (Application) The no effect graph would show that the power reactors have not created conditions that endanger people. All the other graphs indicate change.

11. **(1) A** (Application) The inversely proportional graph would show that as the spill covers more of the bay, less animal life remains. Directly proportional would indicate more animal life with more oil. Oil spills do affect animal life; the leveling off and the peaking and tapering graphs both indicate an increase at the beginning of an action which does not describe an animal population as an oil spill invades.

12. **(4) D** (Application) The temperature rose to a point and increased no further, indicated by the leveling off graph. As the temperature did not continue to change, inversely proportional, directly proportional, and peaking and tapering are eliminated. The no effect graph is eliminated because heating did raise the temperature initially.

13. **(2) 11 years** (Comprehension) The table shows the ever-smaller amount of time it takes to add one billion people to the world population. Since the last one billion people were added in only 12 years, the answer must be a number less than 12. However, the table also shows that since 1960 it's taken at least ten years for one billion people to be added. So the answer should be more than 10. The only choice that is less than 12 and more than 10 is 11 years.

14. **(5) Scientific knowledge is built on previous theories and discoveries.** (Evaluation) The passage describes how a 1596 map led, over time, to the development of the theory of continental drift and plate tectonics. The answer cannot be a detail about the subject. The information does not describe a process of trial and error. The passage also states that the theory of continental drift was proven correct.

15. **(2) the number of Atlantic salmon in a normal, healthy population** (Evaluation) The graph clearly shows that the Atlantic salmon population has been declining since 1975. However, it does not tell you if the 1975 population was exceptionally high to begin with and has just fallen to its more normal level. To know if the 1998 population is dangerously low, you must know the number of salmon in a healthy population.

16. **(4) Eye cataracts are caused by increased exposure to UV light.** (Evaluation) The answer must be about a health effect of UV rays.

17. **(4) Histamine produced by the body in response to allergens causes mucous glands to oversecrete.** (Analysis) Histamine causes mucus membranes to oversecrete, producing nasal drip. The production of mucus is caused by histamine-stimulated glands, not by the nose. Family history does not cause nasal drip. Glands, not capillaries, produce mucus. Avoidance of allergens does not explain why a nasal drip accompanies hay fever.

18. **(3) blenders and mixers** (Application) Blenders and mixers involve motion of parts. All others involve different forms of energy—light, sound, or heat.

19. **(4) amalgam** (Analysis) Of the five mixtures described, only amalgam involves the use of metals.

20. **(3) 14** (Comprehension) Use the right side of the graph (grams per 100 m^3), then follow the bottom temperature until you find 10°C. Look up the 10°C line on the y axis until it is crossed by the curve just beneath the 15 line on the x axis, halfway between 10 and 20 on the right side. Thus, 14 grams is correct. The answer 11 grams is incorrect as it reflects ounces per 1000 ft^3, left side; whereas the question asked for g/100m^3. The graph does not indicate the other answers.

21. **(2) 24** (Analysis) Look at the left side of the graph to find the numbers for 1000 ft^3. Find 44 ounces per ft^3 on the axis and then on the curved line, which crosses 44 at 34° Celsius. Do the same for 12 ounces per ft^3, which crosses at 10° C. Subtract 10 from 34 to arrive at the answer.

22. **(3) the amount of rainfall over cooler regions** (Evaluation) The passage describes the effects of global warming in terms of increased rainfall that is expected to occur over cool regions. Ocean currents and cloud cover do not necessarily address rainfall. As the passage describes the expected rainfall to occur over cool regions, data on hurricanes in the eastern Atlantic and floods in the tropics are not relevant.

23. **(2) The soil in bogs has extremely few nutrients.** (Evaluation) The answer must address why additional nutrients are necessary. The other answer choices do not address the reason insects are essential to the survival of carnivorous plants.

24. **(5) telescope** (Application) In using binoculars, a person is attempting to make an object appear closer, which is what a telescope does. A microscope enlarges small objects. The other tools do not cause objects to appear closer.

25. **(2) oscilloscope** (Application) A heart monitor is used to view the electrical impulses of the heart as visual lines on a screen, which is a type of oscilloscope. None of the other choices turn electricity into lines on a screen.

26. **(1) microscope** (Application) Bacteria are microscopic. In order to verify their presence, they are made to appear larger, but not closer, by using a microscope. None of the other choices magnify. Telescopes make objects appear closer.

27. **(4) spectroscope** (Application) A spectroscope identifies elements by analyzing colored light spectrums. The sun emits light. Other choices may use light but do not break light apart into a spectrum to identify elements.

28. **(2) follow normal eating patterns**
(Comprehension) Tan over blue is normal and requires no deviation from the usual eating pattern. All other choices indicate a change, or action rather than no action. They do not indicate the continuation of normal eating.

29. **(3) biochemistry** (Comprehension) <u>Bio</u>, meaning life, and <u>chemistry</u>, referring to chemicals, would refer to body cells, fluids, and gases. <u>Engeenering</u> refers to chemicals in structures and machines. <u>Astro</u> refers to objects in space such as stars. <u>Inorganic</u> means nonliving. <u>Organic</u> refers to carbon chemicals only.

30. **(3) Light energy travels faster than sound energy.** (Analysis) An explosion produces light energy and sound energy at the same time. If the light energy reaches you first, then it must travel faster. Options 4 and 5 can be ruled out based on personal experience.

31. **(3) 125** (Analysis) The question asks about consequences of a rise in carbon dioxide of four times normal, indicated by the solid line on the graph. The 50 centimeter mark on the left axis intersects the solid graph line above the 125 years mark on the bottom axis, so sea level will rise 50 cm in about 125 years.

32. **(4) filtering pollutants out of drinking water** (Application) The passage describes membranes designed to trap specific substances, and the answer must apply to this trapping or filtering. Osmosis would work for filtering pollutants out of water, but not for the other choices.

33. **(1) because the genetic material from the egg's nucleus must be eliminated** (Application) The diagram shows UV light killing the nucleus of the egg before the skin cell nucleus is inserted. The information given states that a clone has genetic information from only one nucleus—that of the one parent. To allow the nucleus from the parent cell to produce a clone of the parent, the egg's nucleus must be destroyed.

34. **(4) more of all light energy wavelengths** (Analysis) A satellite is above or near the top of Earth's atmosphere. The illustration indicates more light of all wavelengths is received at the top of the atmosphere, not just more infrared light. The sea-level line is beneath the top-of-the-atmosphere line for all wavelengths.

35. **(2) A seismic wave's speed changes as it passes through different materials.** (Analysis) The information explains that it is by measuring the different speeds of seismic waves as they pass through the earth that scientists came to know that Earth's core is made of different substances. Therefore, the waves must travel through different substances at different speeds.

36. **(2) the auditory nerve** (Analysis) The information explains that the cilia are located in the cochlea of the ear. If you locate the cochlea on the diagram, you see that its connection to the brain is via the auditory nerve.

37. **(2) Many hybrids and pure breeds can no longer survive in the wild.** (Evaluation) When humans are unable or choose not to maintain the artificial environment, the hybrids and pure breeds may not survive. It is not harmful that the dog is a friend to humans, that 121 breeds exist, or that desirable traits are fixed. Plants and animals rely on many agents and conditions in evolving; humans are just one more agent and may have prevented extinction in some cases.

38. **(3) crossbreeding** (Application) In crossbreeding, desirable traits are selected, then individuals with those traits are bred in order to produce offspring with the desirable traits. The farmer is using purebreds with the already inbred characteristics he wishes to crossbreed. A hybrid is not yet produced; it is hoped for and will be a result of successful crossbreeding. Hybridization is the result of crossbreeding, while fertilization is any union of egg and sperm and occurs with or without crossbreeding.

39. **(2) a puncture wound while digging in the garden** (Application) Soil and a deep wound are both present in the gardening puncture wound. All the other choices do not indicate both factors.

40. **(4) The DNA in the animal cell is in a nucleus; the virus has no nucleus.** (Comprehension) Find the DNA marked in each cell type and note that the DNA in the animal cell occurs in a nucleus. The viral DNA does not. Nothing in the diagrams indicates the relative amounts of DNA. Also, though the animal cell contains other structures, they are not labeled as DNA helpers. Finally, though both cells have organs for movement, this is not relevant to the question.

41. **(2) An accepted, orderly system aids scientific learning and communication.** (Comprehension) Options 1 and 3 are details that are not supported by the passage. Option 4 is true, but it is neither stated nor implied in the passage. Option 5 contradicts the information given.

42. **(2) 25 percent** (Comprehension) To find the answer, look at the distribution of traits in the Punnett square. For a recessive trait to be expressed, the offspring must have two genes for that trait. Only one of the four squares shows the required two-recessive-gene pair (nn). One out of four is 25 percent.

43. **(4) The climate is actually warming at 2.5° Celsius per century.** (Evaluation) The answer calls for a fact or detail that shows the argument to be faulty. The argument in the passage states that the increase in the sun's energy is solely responsible for global warming, which it describes as an increase of 0.5°C per century. Only option 4 shows this explanation to be inadequate.

44. **(1) In most cases of malaria diagnosed in the United States, the individual contracted the disease outside the U.S. border.** (Analysis) North America is a light area on the map, where malaria has never existed or has been eradicated. Therefore, if a person in the U.S. contracted the disease, it was probably while traveling. Southeast Asia is dark on the map and has a high incidence of malaria. The map does not indicate the direction of the spread of malaria, if any. Cold and temperate areas are not areas of high risk and are not shaded on the map. Much of the earth's densely populated areas are high-risk areas.

45. **(3) conduction and convection** (Application) Heat is flowing from the heating element to the pot by conduction; it is also flowing by conduction from the pot to the water in direct contact with the pot. Within the water, heat is flowing by convection. No other options combine these processes.

46. **(3) It expands its argument from two species to all species.** (Evaluation) The only supporting details for the argument in the passage are the examples of the dodo and the passenger pigeon. It does not follow, therefore, that since human life was not affected by the disappearance of these species, no negative effects will occur if all or most species are allowed to die off.

47. **(5) Unexpected results in experiments often lead to new questions and discoveries.** (Analysis) The question asks you to identify a principle of scientific inquiry, so options 1 and 3 are incorrect. The passage describes how what seemed to be a mistake resulted in a new question, the answer to which the scientists then pursued. In so doing, they made an important discovery.

48. **(2) II** (Analysis) The information explains that the antigen-binding fragments are designed to attach to only one specific antigen. By looking carefully at the diagram, you see that only antigen II has the same shape as the antigen-binding site on the antibody.

49. **(5) Lyme disease is preventable if precautions are taken.** (Analysis) The passage details the carrier, causes, and symptoms of Lyme disease, and explains how people can contract it and avoid it. Option 5 is a conclusion that can be drawn from the information in the passage. All other answer choices provide further details.

50. **(4) It does not address the long-term effects of eating these potatoes.** (Evaluation) The passage implies that because lab animals did not get sick after eating the potatoes for a short time, the potatoes are not harmful to people who may eat them over an entire lifetime. No matter how much the animals ate or what pesticide is used, the study done is inadequate because it was short-term.

SIMULATED TEST B

Pages 71–88

1. **(2) 40 grams** (Application) To get the answer, first find 22°C on the bottom axis, and look to see where each line crosses at this temperature, then subtract to find the difference: 60 – 20 = 40.

2. **(2) tennis ball rolling on a lawn** (Application) The uneven grass surface of a lawn provides far greater friction, or resistance, than any of the other choices. The fuzziness of the tennis ball itself also adds resistance.

3. **(1) La Paz** (Evaluation) La Paz has the lowest boiling temperature of all the locations listed in the table, so it must have the highest altitude.

4. **(3) vegetables cooked in olive oil** (Application) This is the only choice that does not include saturated fats.

5. **(1) rattlesnake bite to a dog** (Application) A rattlesnake bite puts a poisonous liquid in the dog, as does a bee sting. The fish bite, cat bite, heart attack, and accident are not caused by a poisonous liquid.

6. **(4) Up means away from Earth.** (Comprehension) In the illustration, up refers to four different directions, so north, south, east, or west cannot define up. Down means toward the center of Earth and is the opposite of up.

7. **(4) organisms, populations, communities, biosphere** (Analysis) Each item to the right must be more complex than and dependent upon all items to the left. Organisms, populations, communities, biosphere fits the diagram in least complex to the left and most complex to the right. All other options have one or more structures out of order.

8. **(2) the circulatory system** (Application) The diagram shows that a body system is more complex than any of the other options listed.

9. **(1) a dorsal fin** (Application) Dorsal is above and along the backbone; ventral is under the belly; lateral is to the side; caudal refers to the tail only; and posterior refers to a view from behind.

10. **(5) Some seeds are able to survive during long periods of dormancy.** (Analysis) Seeds from pyramid tombs germinating is evidence that some seeds can survive long periods of dormancy. Not all plants can be expected to perform as one example did. There is no reference in the statement to compare or evaluate animal reproduction.

11. **(3) transforms most of its energy into heat** (Application) Since energy is neither created nor destroyed, and you want the greatest amount of energy in the form of heat (to heat your house), it makes the most sense to choose a fuel that turns most of its energy into heat energy as it burns. The other choices yield energy in unwanted forms (light, residue, gas).

12. **(1) The volume of air in the second tube was compressed.** (Evaluation) The fact that the volume of the gas was able to be changed suggests that the atoms within the gas contain empty space. Options 2, 3, 4, and 5 are not related to the concept that atoms have vacuum.

13. **(1) putting PVC containers in a microwave oven** (Application) The passage tells you of two processes that release dangerous PVC from products: chewing and heating. Option 1 is the only choice that satisfies one of these requirements.

14. **(3) to create food for the plant** (Comprehension) The passage states that in photosynthesis the plant makes sugars that help it live and grow: this is the definition of food. The passage does not state that respiration or proteins are involved, nor does it state that sugars are transformed into any other substances. Although the plant does absorb the energy in sunlight during photosynthesis, this absorption is not the purpose, but a part of, the process.

15. **(4) another tribe building a village close by upstream** (Evaluation) A new village upstream would result in pollution of the village's water supply. A new village downstream would not pollute areas upstream. The dye business is assigned to an appropriate area so as not to taint water for personal use. A government school or medical outpost would be forced to use the stream as the village dictates.

16. **(4) Objects are caught in the warp created by the mass of Earth.** (Comprehension) Earth's warp forms a hole in space that traps the objects in it. Air pressure of 14.7 lb./sq. in. is insufficient to keep objects moving at ordinary speeds from escaping into space if no warp existed. The passage and illustrations do not suggest that Earth's spin or magnetism is involved. People can live on any side of Earth.

17. **(3) orbits the sun** (Application) Earth orbits the sun because it is caught in the sun's warp and is not traveling fast enough to escape. The moon is caught in Earth's warp. The other options are not mentioned in the illustration or passage and are not effects of warps.

18. **(4) an astronomer on Earth recording radio signals from radiating stars in the Andromeda Galaxy** (Application) The recording of radio signals which are a form of energy would travel at 186,000 miles per second and not be affected by the warps of the sun, moon, or Earth. In all other options, an object will be moving through one or more warps, so fuel needed, determination of orbital paths, and the escape from and re-entry into space of the object are all affected by the warps.

19. **(2) a greater force than to escape Earth** (Analysis) The greater the mass, the greater the warp. Therefore, the force to escape must be greater. A warp is a hole itself, and escaping the warp is not done by finding a hole in the hole. Escape is determined by speed, not by the mass of the object attempting to escape.

20. **(3) A characteristic that distinguishes a spider from an insect is the number of legs.** (Analysis) Spiders and insects are shown on the graph as having a difference in the number of legs. Birds have wings but not six legs. Only one sea creature is listed, so a generalization about all sea creatures cannot be made. The graph only lists the number of legs and does not give information on the complexity of entire bodies. The graph shows that ungulates (hoofed animals) have four legs, but does not indicate that there are no other animals with four legs.

21. **(2) Sometimes the scientific solution for one problem presents another problem.** (Evaluation) The scientific solution to the farmer's problems presented a problem for the bay's fishing industry. No negative opinions against science, fertilizers, or the farmers were suggested. Using science did solve the original problem. The world's food problems were not discussed in the passage.

22. **(3) maintenance of body temperature** (Analysis) Burning results in heat energy which is evidenced by body temperature. Heat or light, the evidence of burning fuels, is not indicated in any other option.

23. **(4) swish or roll the liquid around the tongue prior to swallowing** (Analysis) Rolling the liquid around the tongue increases the amount and time of exposure to the receptor cells and intensifies the taste. Diluting decreases the concentration as would extra saliva. Swallowing quickly decreases the time on the receptor cells. Holding the nose decreases the inhaling of gases evaporating from the liquid, so the nose cannot heighten the pleasure of the taste.

24. **(3) place the spoon over the back portion of the tongue** (Application) Since the receptors for bitter taste are on the back of the tongue, placing the spoon on top of them prevents much of the liquid from reaching them. All other positions and sucking through a straw force the liquid over the bitter receptors.

25. **(4) Pinus lambertiana** (Application) If the tree has cones, it must be a conifer. If its cones hang down, it must be one of the Pinus trees. If its needles are in bunches of five, it must be a Pinus lambertiana.

26. **(1) increase the proportion of sand** (Application) Water drains easily in sandy soil; thus, adding sand to the clay/loam soil would increase drainage. Increasing clay and decreasing sand would cause the soil to hold more water. Increasing the humus does not increase drainage, nor does the depth of the topsoil.

27. **(4) flower pollination** (Application) To obtain seeds, flowers must be pollinated. Butterflies and moths assist flowers with cross-pollination. Butterfly reproduction would only be important if there were problems in obtaining a large enough butterfly population to pollinate flowers. Chrysalis spinning and apple production would not generally be of interest to a flower seed grower. Butterflies and moths do not destroy worms.

28. **(4) moth** (Analysis) Only moths spin cocoons. Butterflies form a hard chrysalis. Worms and Hymenoptera (bees and ants) do not form cocoons.

29. **(5) arrangement of the atoms** (Analysis) The elements, formulas, and number of hydrogen and carbon atoms in isobutane and normal butane are the same; only the arrangement is different. Therefore, the difference in boiling points is likely due to the difference in arrangement.

30. **(4) time, size, mass, string thickness, and distance of pull** (Comprehension) The time, size, mass, string thickness, and distance of pull were the same for each pendulum. The length of the string was the variable being tested. In the scientific method, an experiment must have only one variable. All other factors must be controlled.

31. **(3) the length of the string** (Analysis) The length of the string was different for every pendulum. It is the only variable which indicates the factor being tested and the hypothesis that defines the test. Ball size, mass, and distance of pull were all controlled.

32. **(3) dependent on the length of the string** (Analysis) The results show that the shorter the string length, the more swings per minute. Thus, the number of swings per unit of time is dependent on string length. The mass of the balls and the thickness of string could not affect the swings, as they were the same for each pendulum. The results were not constant, and since string length was varied, the results cannot be considered independent.

33. **(4) whole blood** (Evaluation) If you examine the amounts of potassium and sodium needed in each type of cell, you see that the maximum difference in the distribution for each substance in whole blood is only 40 mg/100 g. The difference in distribution is greater for all other cell types in the table.

34. **(4) In mitosis, daughter cells have the same DNA as the parent cell.** (Comprehension) The passage explains that DNA in the parent cell is exactly copied, or replicated, during mitosis. Each exact copy goes into a daughter cell. Option 1 is incorrect because each daughter cell gets a complete copy of the parent cell's DNA. Options 2, 3, and 5 include concepts not mentioned in the passage.

35. **(3) the randomness implied by quantum theory** (Evaluation) Einstein compares quantum uncertainty with "playing dice," a game of chance, in which the outcome is uncertain, or random. None of the other choices addresses the "dice" metaphor that Einstein uses.

36. **(5) 828.96 inches per minute** (Analysis) A point on the record's rim travels 33 revolutions per minute. The record's radius is 4 inches, so 33 revolutions/minute x 2π r = 66 π/minute x 4 inches = 828.96 inches per minute.

37. **(3) 10** (Analysis) Uranium 238 has 92 protons (as seen from the bottom axis); lead has 82 protons; 92 – 82 = 10.

38. **(2) Cathode rays can be bent by a magnetic field.** (Analysis) In experiment A, the ray flows directly across the length of the tube. Yet in B, when a magnet is place near the tube, it causes the rays to bend toward it, thus showing clearly that the rays can be bent by the magnetic field created by a magnet.

39. **(3) stop eating chicken from factory farms** (Application) The passage tells you that eating meat puts too many antibiotics in your body and that chickens are routinely given large doses of antibiotics. Option 1 is incorrect because the flu is not treated with antibiotics, and the subject is not addressed in the passage. The passage does not imply that you should avoid needed medications or that the antibiotics are not also in chicken eggs. The passage explains that feeding chickens antibiotics is done routinely and not because they are ill.

40. **(2) Magnetic north has not always been in the same place.** (Analysis) The passage states that recent undersea lava flows in the direction of magnetic north. So if earlier lava flows point in a direction different from today's magnetic north, then magnetic north must have been at a different location in the past. All the other options are details from the passage.

41. **(5) the neutron** (Comprehension) The only difference shown between an atom of hydrogen and its two isotopes is the neutrons in the nucleus.

42. **(2) pesticides** (Comprehension) The passage states that organically grown products are raised without the use of chemicals. Pesticides are agricultural chemicals, so they would not be in organic products. There is nothing to suggest harvesting equipment would not be used or that water must be filtered. Both compost and fertilizer can be made without artificial chemicals.

43. **(5) Red Sea** (Analysis) The higher the salinity, the more likely the sea is in a hot, dry region. Of the seas listed in the chart, the Red Sea has the highest salinity (40 ppt).

44. **(4) stricter standards for drinking water safety** (Evaluation) Option 4 is the only option that describes a public health measure. Options 1, 2, and 5 address health care for individuals. Option 3 addresses public health but suggests eliminating a worthwhile public health measure.

45. **(4) the effects of malathion on human health** (Evaluation) The spraying was done to protect human health against mosquitoes carrying West Nile virus. Yet to fully support this argument, it must be shown that malathion itself—a pesticide that kills living things—is not equally or more harmful than the virus.

46. **(1) Oil and gasoline are fossil fuels.** (Evaluation) The passage states that fuel cells were originally intended as a pollution-free, alternative source of energy. The passage concludes that using oil and gas for hydrogen production in fuel cells undermines the original purpose of fuel-cell technology. The fact that oil and gasoline are fossil fuels supports this conclusion.

47. **(3) analysis of patterns in historical records** (Comprehension) Walker analyzed decades of global weather records to find patterns that eventually led to his conclusion. The passage does not say he did field work or experiments. His conclusions were based on evidence, not abstract theories.

48. **(3) Insects are valuable as plant pollinators.** (Comprehension) The passage uses the yucca moth, the only insect that pollinates the yucca plant, as an example of why insects are important and should be preserved. The conservation of insects is the main idea of the passage, and the example used illustrates that insects are important as pollinators. The passage does not discuss which species evolved first or if the insect has a natural predator. The passage does not imply that insect preserves should be established.

49. **(5) Some scientific evidence points to the possibility that dinosaurs and birds are closely related.** (Comprehension) The passage describes evidence that demonstrates a close connection between birds and dinosaurs. Option 1 is too general. Option 2 directly contradicts the information in the passage. Options 3 and 4 are details that are stated or implied within the passage.

50. **(2) the electrical field** (Evaluation) The diagram shows that only after passing through the electrical field (indicated by (+) on one side and (–) on the other) do the rays separate into individual rays.

SCIENCE

Name: _____ Class: _____ Date: _____

○ Simulated Test A   ○ Simulated Test B

1 ① ② ③ ④ ⑤	11 ① ② ③ ④ ⑤	21 ① ② ③ ④ ⑤	31 ① ② ③ ④ ⑤	41 ① ② ③ ④ ⑤
2 ① ② ③ ④ ⑤	12 ① ② ③ ④ ⑤	22 ① ② ③ ④ ⑤	32 ① ② ③ ④ ⑤	42 ① ② ③ ④ ⑤
3 ① ② ③ ④ ⑤	13 ① ② ③ ④ ⑤	23 ① ② ③ ④ ⑤	33 ① ② ③ ④ ⑤	43 ① ② ③ ④ ⑤
4 ① ② ③ ④ ⑤	14 ① ② ③ ④ ⑤	24 ① ② ③ ④ ⑤	34 ① ② ③ ④ ⑤	44 ① ② ③ ④ ⑤
5 ① ② ③ ④ ⑤	15 ① ② ③ ④ ⑤	25 ① ② ③ ④ ⑤	35 ① ② ③ ④ ⑤	45 ① ② ③ ④ ⑤
6 ① ② ③ ④ ⑤	16 ① ② ③ ④ ⑤	26 ① ② ③ ④ ⑤	36 ① ② ③ ④ ⑤	46 ① ② ③ ④ ⑤
7 ① ② ③ ④ ⑤	17 ① ② ③ ④ ⑤	27 ① ② ③ ④ ⑤	37 ① ② ③ ④ ⑤	47 ① ② ③ ④ ⑤
8 ① ② ③ ④ ⑤	18 ① ② ③ ④ ⑤	28 ① ② ③ ④ ⑤	38 ① ② ③ ④ ⑤	48 ① ② ③ ④ ⑤
9 ① ② ③ ④ ⑤	19 ① ② ③ ④ ⑤	29 ① ② ③ ④ ⑤	39 ① ② ③ ④ ⑤	49 ① ② ③ ④ ⑤
10 ① ② ③ ④ ⑤	20 ① ② ③ ④ ⑤	30 ① ② ③ ④ ⑤	40 ① ② ③ ④ ⑤	50 ① ② ③ ④ ⑤

Copyright © 2002 by Steck-Vaughn Company. *GED Science Exercise Book*. Permission granted to reproduce for classroom use.